...IN A NUTSHELL

...in a Nutshell
Copyright © 2023 by Larry Johnston

All rights reserved. No part of this book may be used or reproduced in any form, electronic or mechanical, including photocopying, recording, or scanning into any information storage and retrieval system, without written permission from the author except in the case of brief quotation embodied in critical articles and reviews.

Printed in the United States of America
The Troy Book Makers • Troy, New York • thetroybookmakers.com

To order additional copies of this title,
contact your favorite local bookstore
or visit www.shoptbmbooks.com

ISBN: 978-1-61468-830-3

...IN A NUTSHELL

essays and real-life stories

Larry Johnston

For June, Mark and Marly

Contents

Preface 1

I. Essays 3

   Proceed At Your Own Risk 5

   Handwritten Notes vs. Texting 6

   Misconceptions 7

   The NEVER-TOO-LATE School Reunion 9

   Giving 11

   Wardrobe Wars 12

   Airheads versus Black Ice 13

   Thank You Waldo 14

   A New Theory of Relativity 15

   The Independence Gene 16

   Speed Demons 17

   Curiosity 18

   No News is Good News 20

   A Lesson from Dr. King 22

   Three Little Questions 24

   Our Pandemic Heroes 26

   Good Taste 28

L'Amour Pour L'Armoire 30

Zappy Birthday 32

Labels 33

Our Unknown Hero 35

Mutiny Without Bounty 38

Coulda, Woulda, Shoulda 40

Brains 41

The Golf Panacea 42

Foibles 45

Penny and Charlie 46

Just in Time 47

Caring 49

Comfortable 50

II. Real-life Stories 51

Worst Case Scenario: Our First House 53

A "Little Place" in the Country 73

The Mysterious, Misunderstood
and Mismanaged Restaurant Business 97

...One More Thought 130

Preface

I understand that something called a preface should appear on the initial pages of a book. I have no idea how to write one of these things. However, it is important for you to know that this is not a traditional book. It really is a call to arms. Arms that hug. It is written with the belief that we all yearn to share our concerns, our wishes, and our humanity.

. . . in a Nutshell is comprised of two sections. The first is a collection of essays that were primarily written during the pandemic, a time allotted for reflection. These essays have no common denominator except their willingness to get to the heart of matters. They try to understand human conditions and the humor that goes with them. No serious conclusions, just observations. The second section contains several real-life experiences of our family in dealing with abandoned or neglected buildings and turning them into homes. And finally, a story about this author's unlikely adventures into restaurant ownership. Hopefully, these stories will provide you with enough background information to help understand the mentality that prompted the writing of essays.

A preface should encourage you to proceed on a well-informed basis. In this spirit, my first essay contains a warning about what you can expect. Good friends behave in this manner.

Part I

Essays

· Proceed At Your Own Risk ·

You are about to engage in an experiment. Over the past decade, and especially during the pandemic, I found writing to be a positive means of expressing thoughts and recording events. Nothing too serious, but similar to creating photo albums to capture memories. Recently, there have been suggestions to place these writings into a blog or a pod, whatever those things are. This option will never happen. The big black hole posing as an internet is not a place for intimacy. Words need to breathe. They belong on paper. Writing comes with a promise of honesty and consideration of the human condition. Laughter at oneself is always a good idea. This little collection of stories comes with a pledge to talk plainly about the essence of matters. Hence, the title ... *in a Nutshell*.

To deal with the possibility of going forward, I arranged for a meeting with my id and ego. My id had a history of missing critical meetings, and my ego had never been a rock to build upon. Bringing these two unreliable forces together was always a gamble.

I thought that this meeting was a good idea. They thought otherwise. Immediately, they saw the problems of introducing a human being whose behavior was unpredictable, who had no apparent expertise in any subject, possessed a short attention span, was skeptical of anything hi-tech and, finally, a person who maintained a closet full of little contrarian views. This meant that they were attempting to support someone whose only experience involves matters of the heart and soul.

My id raised red flags about my unpredictability. My ego advised me never to do this kind of thing again and asked for copies of the minutes of the meeting. Both asked for hold harmless agreements. One alarmist and one wimp. Some friends.

Armed with neither support nor rational thinking, the only logical answer was ... full speed ahead. For sure, we will find out if this was a good idea.

Each one of us will be proceeding at our own risk.

· Handwritten Notes vs. Texting ·

C'mon, admit it. We all love to open an envelope addressed to us by another human being. It means that someone has been caring enough to think about us. To let us know how they feel, what they wish for us or just thanking us. The effort is a handshake, the words inside are a hug. Try hugging a text.

We know that communication is a sensitive topic. It is always risky to talk about "the good old days". Believe it or not, we older folks clearly remember when we were kids. One of our favorite ways of expressing ourselves was sticking a finger down our throats and mimicking vomiting whenever being lectured by an adult. What did adults know about anything?

Today, there is a basic conflict in communication. Speed versus substance. Elders never want to compete on the basis of speed. There is zero interest in such a contest. Trying to work with those ridiculous little keys on such a small hand-held device is unnatural and dehumanizing. There is additional anxiety that your message will never reach the intended party. Also, just the sheer volume of messaging means that potentially thoughtful words will be drowned in a sea of gigabytes. This is not a dignified way for meaningful words to disappear.

On the topic of substance, elders win. Just compare the seconds needed for texting with the thoughtfulness of written notes. But the big winner is the fact that we are attempting to express emotions. Intimacy is verboten in the gigabyte world. Important things like love, yearnings or congratulations are forged in handwriting.

This little story is not a lecture. Texting is a great tool for staying in touch. However, occasionally it might be fun to express yourself more intimately in writing. It could be adventurous. The receiver of such a strange form of communication may not even know how to respond.

So what?

· Misconceptions ·

I just looked at a video of my life. What a mess! So many misconceptions. I came into this party as a blank page. All this clutter must have been the work of others. Who permitted this to happen? My parents? Teachers? Friends? All the above? None of the above? Every human being on this planet carries misconceptions around on their journey, most of them readily adopted because we trusted the sources.

Looking around for answers, the first item that cropped up was our parents, our very first contacts with humanity. Of course, this meant that we really had little or no input as to the validity of the information being passed on. We've since learned that at this stage of life, parents are ill-equipped to convey information in a precise or orderly fashion. As new parents ourselves, we learned this simple truth. The hard way. All the pressures of dealing with little kids who are always running around willy-nilly necessarily means that parents' instructions and teaching skills are neither well-thought-out nor appropriate. This is not the time for wisdom, we are all just trying to survive. As a result of this hectic environment, parents cannot realistically be blamed for misconceptions. As a matter of fact, these little errors may have been taught by prior parents. With some families there is the very real possibility that many of these misconceptions were generational, passed on almost religiously from parents to children. Especially stories about heredity, and revealing tales of possible scoundrels, male and female. We should agree that this category of misconceptions is unique to families.

The fun starts with education through high school, where we are left in a whirlpool of teachers with differing styles and degrees of respect. Here, teachers were operating within well-known guidelines. There's also the playground, sports, and after school friendships where so-called facts were being loosely distributed. Sometime, just try and remember the impact that this stage had in planting misconceptions. It is unlikely that we would be able to pinpoint specific cases where information was erroneous at the time. However, as the following years unfolded, we undoubtedly would be unearthing misconceptions that were rooted in this naive stage.

This takes us into so-called adulthood, including some who might attend college. This is the scary place where accountability finally comes into the picture. The years of being young adults are critical. A time for the training wheels to come off, with minds free at last. It is really beyond any mortal's ability to describe the variety of both teachings and impressions that are compressed into these years. A barrage of new ideas, concepts, and opinions, all fighting for survival in the real world. Does this sound familiar?

A lifetime of corrections. More time spent weeding out misconceptions than planting seeds.

Welcome to being a human being.

· The NEVER-TOO-LATE School Reunion ·

I'm not really a reunion guy. The high school variety were never experienced. I did attend a 10th college reunion, but the chemistry of the years 18 to 21 somehow failed to reignite. The exception to this behavior is the fact that I do stay in touch with a few college classmates and greatly value the ongoing honesty and support exchanged in these special friendships.

However, here's a real reunion story.

I decided to call a friend that I knew in grammar school well over seventy years ago.

We graduated together from the 6th grade in 1947. Now, that's a real gamble, based on the hope that a special bond takes place at that age. We were "buddies" in the old-fashioned sense, running around footloose, playing in sports, raising a little hell. You know. It was a great age.

Why did I decide to call Charlie? I had been talking with some friends about the game of golf and remembered that a number of years ago, I read somewhere that he had won some golf tournaments in his part of the world. At that time, my life was busy and complex, and it never occurred to me to give him a call.

I found a number via white pages and dialed, not knowing what to expect. A woman answered.

I said "Hi", gave her my full name and stated that I went to grammar school with Charlie. "We graduated together in 1947." Good for Charlie's wife. She didn't hang up. Instead, I heard her calling out to him, "There's some guy on the phone who claims he went to school with you over seventy years ago."

Suspense. He came to phone and not only knew who I was, but immediately began to give me a hard time, saying, "Where did you disappear to?" This was wonderful. Only friends with a solid base talk this way to each other. He went on to say that, back then, I was his best friend. That's a statement that most people don't hear in a lifetime. I certainly hadn't. He then said, "Why did you suddenly move away without consulting me?" I had no excuse. I couldn't even remember much, if anything, about the years immediately after sixth grade. Well, in our 80's, reaching that far back in memories is like wandering around in a smoky room.

We did laugh about some of the different incidents that we each recalled, proving that individuals store things independently. We covered a few topics, including our mutual lifetime interest in the game of golf. I mentioned that I had written a little piece about the game and he asked me to forward a copy. I agreed. This was a small step in keeping our contact alive.

We then exchanged some emails and raised the possibility of getting together. Pretty wild. Two old guys living many miles apart, talking about directions via highways that didn't even exist over seventy years ago, wondering if a meeting place we recalled was even still in existence. Simple logistics? Not really. We picked a place that, hopefully, was still there. With cautious spousal endorsement, we planned our reunion.

We met in the coffee shop of a suburban hotel. The first hurdle was recognizing one another. Surprisingly, we knew right away who the other guy was. There must be some mysterious bonds that cut through the issue of physical appearance. Interestingly, we are both about the same height and weight. Same deal as age twelve.

The reunion was amazing. We didn't know where to start, but this was understandable given the time span. We talked about ensuing school years, families, business experiences and other highlights. For me, the most interesting discovery was the fact that we both emphasized incidents that were "turning points" in our lives. These were primarily adverse happenings that instilled either new awareness or determination. Heartfelt revelations. Good stuff.

We both had to adjourn. How to handle the next step, if any? We left with a hug, and an intention to somehow meet again. Maybe even getting to play a round of golf together. How great would that be? We'll see.

I believe that we were both delighted to have met again. I also believe that friendships of this magnitude are to be treasured.

It's never too late.

· Giving ·

Looking for guidance? We all are. To conduct this search, we must be daring enough to look into our innermost thoughts. This involves objectively (hah!) evaluating our experiences. This storehouse of memories comes with attached emotions, ranging from sadness to exhilaration. However, there is always one trait that these recollections share. They are transient ... they come and go. If we are lucky, however, we may discover that there is one category of memories that always delivers positive and lasting feelings ... those that involved acts of giving. These recollections are so powerful that they make other experiences seem trivial.

Let's be honest. We spend a lot of our time worrying about our own welfare. In this mode, we may also feel twinges of guilt. It is disconcerting to realize that such self-centered activities may not provide the satisfaction and consistency that we anticipated. Oftentimes, it is easy to blame these disappointments on the fact that we are living in an increasingly complex and demanding world.

However, even on our worst days, when we engage in an act of giving, we derive a sense of worth. This giving could be as simple as an expression of concern for someone's welfare or an offer of assistance. At such times, we may have considered these acts of giving as merely normal behavior. Actually, they were heaven sent. Just name one of our everyday activities that has such extraordinary power. Simple, honest and potentially inspirational. For both the giver and the recipient.

One of the other interesting things about giving is the fact that, oftentimes, it is our own little secret. These anonymous happenings can be one of the most enticing attractions to giving. They are special opportunities to do something that is so praiseworthy without praise. The simplest giving can be a gesture, the grandest would be the sacrifice of one's life for the lives of others. In between, it can be anything from consoling others, offering a helping hand or teaching a lesson.

Giving.

It costs nothing, yet is priceless.

· Wardrobe Wars ·

Women win. They are smarter than men, and even live longer just to prove it. They also have greater selections in clothing. Just enter any major department store and you are immediately struck with the disproportionate amount of space dedicated to women's wardrobes. This is perfectly appropriate. On the flip side, space allocated for the sale of gentlemen's clothing has been cleverly hidden.

Men neither deserve nor expect clothiers to lose money on their behalf. It is perfectly understandable that the amount of space dedicated to this losing proposition has consistently been reduced over the years. It is obvious that once men stopped wearing suits, the industry was doomed to a spiraling downward trend and did not warrant valuable space in department stores. After all the fuss about wearing formal clothes as suits and ties, everything would de-escalate down to shirts and pants. That's not enough demand to excite any clothier. The pants alone are a nightmare. Our waistlines are in never-ending battles with width and length. This is due to either expansion or slippage of waistlines, mostly outward and even downward. Waists used to be somewhere around the bottom of the ribcage, but now are anywhere south. Therefore, because of these moving parts, men have a terrible time selecting waist and length sizes with any degree of accuracy. This means that buying pants is never an enjoyable pastime.

Men have always treasured only one favorite article of clothing and that is dungarees. Nowadays, they happen to be sold as "jeans", but that doesn't change the fact that pants made from denim are both rugged and comfortable. Manufacturers, in their desire to make men buy more of these items, have played around with gimmicky changes such as making them look already broken-in or slimming down the legs. These modifications have not only alienated customers but have further stressed the tenuous relationship that has existed between clothiers and men. This unfortunate tug-of-war may threaten the survival of men's departments in large stores. So be it. Most of us would be happy with the good old Army and Navy stores. What ever happened to them?

It's terrific that women continue to be fashionable and look great. The wonderful relationship that exists between women, designers and department stores should continue to flourish. Everyone seems to love one another.

· Airheads versus Black Ice ·

What's the big deal about "black ice"? Here in the northeast, we are constantly and annoyingly being warned to avoid these hidden patches of disaster. From November all the way through April.

We airheads pay no attention.

Let's set the record straight ... black ice is not black. It is invisible.

Black ice accidents are sometimes called "slip and fall" episodes, especially when insurance is involved. In our little story, this airhead was carrying objects in both hands going down steps outside the back door when I ventured onto the invisible ice. I became airborne. Flying backward. Without hands or wrists to break the fall, the back of my head became my landing gear. This maneuver should really be called "slip and fly".

What followed was shock, disbelief, guilt and humility. How could anyone be this stupid? I'm woozy, the back of my head is bleeding, but I manage to crawl back into the house. My wonderful wife, who earlier had warned me to watch out for the black ice, ran to my rescue. She had the good grace to neither scold nor chuckle, having witnessed my many adventures of this type. Knowing my advanced years, it was a good idea to call 911.

The first responders were professional and understanding. Apparently, they have seen quite a few stubborn elderly men who engage in slip and fly activity. They mentioned that, oddly, they never seem to experience these airborne episodes with women. As they were loading me into the ambulance, I overheard my wife warning them to watch out for the black ice. They chuckled.

The emergency room staff was also wonderful and well versed in treating us old black ice flyers. A kindly nurse told me not to worry, because all men are "hard-headed" and somehow handle these blows to the head quite well. The attending physician then placed some stitches in my scalp, careful not to go too deep and let some of the air escape. The ER staff then gave me a fond farewell, knowing full well that they would be seeing me again.

Airheads are repeat offenders.

· Thank You Waldo ·

Ralph Waldo Emerson was a genius. He used to hang around with some pretty smart people, like Henry Thoreau and Margaret Fuller. They were essayists, an informal think tank that exchanged ideas in the mid 1800s. Their deliberations generally produced substance rather than the kind of puff pieces that float around within today's intelligentsia. These individuals understood the essence of the real world, nature and the precious value of common sense. Emerson preferred to be known as "Waldo", which tells you a lot about his rebellious nature. Just consider his take on success, and you will understand the clarity of his thinking. Also, you may yearn for the type of concise and meaningful analysis that is sorely missed in today's dialogue. Waldo was not impressed with titles or awards. Thank you, Waldo, for the following:

What is success?

> To laugh often and much; to win the respect of intelligent people and affection of children; to earn the appreciation of honest critics and endure the betrayal of false friends; to appreciate beauty; to find the best in others; to leave the world a bit better, whether by a healthy child, a garden patch, or a redeemed social condition; to know even one life has breathed easier because you have lived.

This is to have succeeded!

This quotation requires just one point of clarification. Where Waldo talks about a "healthy child", he is not suggesting perfection, he is referring to a child that actually survived the trauma of childbirth. Infant mortality was rampant in that era and it was reason to be thankful when this danger was overcome.

Waldo's words cut to the heart.

Try them on for size.

· A New Theory of Relativity ·

Relatives ... you inherit them. It's not a selection process and there are no interviews. If you're lucky enough to get married, you obtain twice the number of relatives as a bonus. A whole batch of new people come with the deal. Should you decide to stay single you have to play with the cards you were dealt. Whatever your status, relatives hang on, and will probably outlive you. They come in all flavors, some yummy, others not so much.

With marriage, the in-law expansion seems to be unlimited. Because they are called in-laws, do they, by law, carry along with themselves their coterie of relatives? Is there a screening process where the principals involved get a chance to meet or at least observe this new wing of their family? If you don't get along with the in-laws, is there a law that requires a workout concession? Well, let's not stay too long on the topic of in-laws. We already have our hands full with our primary bunch. Our family. This wonderful group alone can be challenging. Aside from the founding mother and father you may have brothers and sisters, lots of uncles and aunts and cousins galore. And of course, the grandparents, the nicest ones of all. Technically, everyone is "family", but due to geography and sheer numbers there are some that will always remain a mystery and must be treated as "distant relatives". We intentionally are leaving out the "step" variety, those rare creatures that are unexpected additions to the main branches of the family tree.

Families should always be treated as gifts. They deserve our ongoing love.

However, there's only one important fact we must always remember ... they inherited you.

· The Independence Gene ·

Every human being on this planet is born with an independence gene.

It appears with your first breath and continues with those first steps. At ages two through three it shows up as a noisy rebellion against authority. It shifts into high gear again during the early teen years, notable for its frequency of clashes with adults. Although it simmers through higher education where mixed messages are delivered, the independence gene remains intact and empowers our survival in the real world.

It never goes away.

The ongoing presence of the independence gene manifests itself throughout history. How else do we account for the ongoing birth of resistance movements wherever corrupt or powerful forces attempt to rob us of our liberty? The independence gene is always alerted and becomes activated in these circumstances.

This dominant force un-masks political ideologies that disguise themselves as "peoples" movements but are always run by totalitarians. These systems are dishonest at their core, unable to fulfill promises and structured to dictate how we should live. Doctrinaire or authoritarian governing never works.

The independence gene is your guardian angel.

No matter where you are born or where you live.

· Speed Demons ·

Normal human beings should not be impressed by warp speed. We know that life is only beautiful when played at a nice tempo. Like a waltz, or even a fox trot. We see everyone frantically trying to catch up to the latest speed devils. These speed demons-from-hell are making our lives faster, but less substantive. The latest frenzy that produced 5G is just a harbinger. When will 6G or even 7 and 8Gs come flying into our lives? So what? Of course, there are exceptions where dynamic speed is critical, such as the urgency to manufacture warships and airplanes with the outbreak of World War II in the early 1940s. And recently, the unprecedented necessity to quickly develop a vaccination to battle a pandemic. Heroic speed is required in times of crisis.

However, in everyday life, our high-tech giants don't have any idea when or where their races to the warp speed finish line will end. Does their current portfolio of products provide any insight regarding their true business goals? Are they designed to make life faster? Easier? Or just planned obsolescence? While their current offerings may be clothed in the garb of normal business practices, their actual objective is sinister. It has become apparent that their real goal is dependency.

They have already achieved phase one. Their little handheld devices have become so essential that, without one, we can barely get through a single day. The next chapter is collection of data, which is already well underway. Just look up any single name or topic and the overwhelming collection of data that spills out is enough to frighten everyone.

If thinking about any of these increasingly powerful influences in our lives is troublesome, we should remember that traditional human behavior is on our side. We will never be good robots. We just have way too many working parts.

Neither speed nor dependency carry substance, the true measure of life.

Listen to your heart and common sense.

They obey speed limits.

· Curiosity ·

We are all born with inquisitive minds. Curiosity is the engine that helps us solve problems, gather information, become enlightened and create inventions. However, even something as normal as curiosity comes with reasonable parameters. When overzealous, it can be harmful. You know, the kind of activity that allegedly kills cats. The mind-your-own-business type of activity.

This little story will dare to talk only about a specific brand of curiosity that normally arises after we sell a home to people we never met before. This phenomenon is engendered by our natural interest in the welfare of both the residents and the property that we have just sold to these unsuspecting strangers. A universal logical question after the closing is, "How are they going to like the place that we loved and/or tolerated?" They may have looked like nice people at the closing but looks can be deceptive. We also knew that there had been an inspection and the traditional "walk through" before the closing. But these events are like rehearsals for school plays back in the 6th grade ... no one really pays attention. Buyers are usually too smitten with getting their hands on the property. Sellers just want to get through these final hurdles.

After these closings, anxieties shift to the sellers. We begin to experience troubling thoughts about the welfare of the new owners. We start to wonder what happens when they start to uncover our little secrets. Our so-called improvements, all those little quirks? If you've never entertained this type of curiosity, stop reading. You are not the type of person that we are familiar with. Please don't tell us that you left the place in picture perfect condition and were never tempted to call and find out how things were going. Human beings without this nagging curiosity are either saints or disillusioned.

Over the years we experienced the curiosity syndrome each time we were the sellers of a house, or even a co-op. However, when we sold our very first house, our curiosity factor was stronger since it had been an abandoned horse stable that we converted into a residence, and there might be concerns about the condition of the structure. We carried this curiosity around for 25 years and finally found the courage to call the owners. We had done some research and had found that the same owners were still living there and had decided to build a new house on the existing property. Apparently, they believed that the setting and privacy deserved such an investment. Over the years we had occasions to be in the area and had taken peeks down the driveway and, sure enough, there was a nice new house. This gave us the additional courage to contact the owners.

Thankfully, they were not only receptive, but even encouraged us to visit. We did plan such an event and brought our adult children along to find out whether their recollections of the property matched ours. Our hosts were rightfully proud of the design and quality of their new home. However, we were sufficiently curious and brave enough to ask about the old structures. The big surprise was the revelation that they loved the home as purchased but needed more space for their planned larger family. They decided to build a third floor on top of our existing two floors. They had even obtained all the necessary building permits to do so. Well, as the project got underway and while the third-floor addition was being framed, the entire building collapsed!!! What??? We were shocked and chagrined. Was this due to our shoddy work, our amateur undertaking? Graciously, they admitted that such a project was solely their decision and proved to be overly ambitious.

This meeting was memorable in that it certainly addressed the normally troublesome curiosity factor. However, it also was both shocking and historical (hysterical?). We discovered that a place where we had devoted long hours to convert to living quarters became exhausted and just laid down and quit.

Has this experience frightened you enough to never contact a new owner?

· No News is Good News ·

The term "media" is not synonymous with an old-fashioned thing called "The News".

Once upon a time there was something called the Fourth Estate, an enterprise dedicated to keeping governments and elected officials in line. Impartial, honest, and diligent. The original intent of this profession was to serve as watchdogs on our behalf. Where and when did this wonderful concept evolve into the mess that we now call The Media?

As senior citizens, we have the luxury of recalling an era when reports coming over the airways actually sounded like real news. With radio, we had heroes like Edward R. Morrow and H.V. Kaltenborn. The early days of TV had similar megastars, such as Walter Cronkite and Huntley & Brinkley. With hindsight, even these larger-than-life broadcasters may have had subtle agendas, but their presentations were largely accepted at face value. It has been all downhill since this reputable timeframe. Enter the explosion of television cable shows, talk radio and, recently, a stampede of unreliable blurbs streaming out of the internet, this generation's genie. We can't even consider the internet as a credible "news" source. It's not only an insult to our intelligence, but borders on being immoral when portrayed as a reliable source of factual news.

What are we to do? For openers, let's discuss the topic of bias. It's no secret that we usually gravitate to a TV station, newspaper or other source whose political philosophy most closely matches our own. That's OK, but let's not pretend that their work is straightforward. Ideology rules the day, tilted at the behest of the organization that owns the enterprise. Just look at the editorials in the newspapers and at the TV headlines to receive a clear picture concerning their political preferences. Again, that's OK. We pick our own poison.

The problem lies outside of the newspaper editorial pages and the TV shows that feature opinionated personalities. Here, we run into disturbing evidence that the actual news can be slanted. Most of the techniques to alter the news are subtle in nature. One fairly common practice is deletion of critical facts which change the meaning, or the significance of the subject being covered. This is the type of egregious behavior that should not be tolerated. Of course, there's the fairly well-known practice of "squashing" or "burying" news. Important facts that the readership or audience never reads or hears. These activities are reprehensible.

The obvious remedy is to have all media entities openly declare their commitment to present factual news despite their obvious political preferences that are stated on their editorial pages and opinion-oriented tv shows. We urgently need clear statements that their news reporting will always be fact-checked and consistently adhere to honest principles of journalism. This assurance should be in bold face print, stating that the news segments of their offerings hold to the highest standards of their profession. We could even begin to think of them as the "Fourth Estate". Maybe even as "Watchdogs".

Wouldn't that be nice?

· A Lesson from Dr. King ·

He would tell us that we have failed to take an honest look at ourselves.

It's embarrassing. And sad. And hurtful. How did we manage to arrive at this point in history having such a basic misunderstanding of what makes Americans tick? The only one who happened to get it right is Dr. Martin Luther King. His insight correctly identified content of character as the proper judge of human behavior. While his statement involved racial consideration, in his heart he knew that character, in fact, is the only true measure in all that we do. When was the last time we heard any so-called leader or political party espouse character as the prerequisite that should guide our destiny?

The "content" of our national character has somehow grown into a mixed bag of ideologies, none of them clearly or honestly stated. They are patched-together platforms, mostly designed to win elections rather than plot a course that reflects the true character and aspirations of our country. How do we get back on track? Perhaps the best place to start is to reacquaint ourselves with the basic traits that have defined the true American character since our founding:

Independent Spirit

The ignition that started the engine, prompting human beings to leave the security of their homelands, venture to an unknown land and, once there, deciding to fight for freedom from tyranny. We occasionally see this spirit emerge when States claim that a central government is treading on their rights or when individuals or groups are being treated unfairly. Thankfully, these incidents provide evidence that our heritage of having an independent spirit remains an irrepressible part of our character.

Toughness

Think pioneer grit. Think about the bravery of our armed forces. How many Americans today are aware of the courage, fortitude and determination of these settlers and warriors who faced hardships that are inconceivable in today's culture? While it is encouraging to know that individual acts of courage take place in thousands of lives every day, this trait does not exist as a guiding component of our national character. We need to have the toughness of our forbearers when deciding to take the more difficult path rather than the easy road.

Accountability

Taking responsibility for one's actions was the norm. When did we start blaming others for our actions or predicaments? Whenever we see a pattern of shirking responsibility, warning signals should be set off alerting us that we are headed in the wrong direction. When the message of victimhood is preached, it erodes the fabric of our character. This mindless practice serves no positive purpose and has the unhealthy result of dividing our populace. Being accountable is a prerequisite of having good character.

Compassion

By far, our best and most enduring character trait. Each day, untold numbers of our citizens perform acts of kindness and heroism to help their fellow human beings. Witness our behavior following natural disasters, where we rush to the aid of the stricken, both here and abroad. Our charities, volunteers and religious groups are active and effective, fueled by an ongoing desire to provide a helping hand. This very special attribute must continue be at the heart of our national character. However, we must be wise in seeing that our compassionate efforts actually achieve long lasting positive results rather than creating false expectations.

Commitment

We must replenish and commit to uphold these national principles. It is apparent that our independent spirit and compassionate nature remain important strengths and sources of inspiration for managing our destiny. Regarding our toughness, we need to address a troubling tendency to delay hard decisions on security and financial matters that threaten our well being. And, lastly, it is critical for us to restore accountability as a prerequisite for all individuals who are entrusted to hold public office.

Dr. King would encourage us to judge our character.

Let's make him proud of us.

· Three Little Questions ·

1942. It was our first day in the first grade. A Catholic school. We were a typical group of kids. Newly minted graduates of kindergarten. Know-it-alls. Dressed up in grown-up clothes. Nervous, but not enough to keep us from fidgeting around and kidding with new friends. Attention spans of black-capped chickadees. Then she came into the room, dressed in an outfit that was very different from our recent kindergarten teachers. She smiled and it lit up the room. She gave us her name, which was really two names, a girl and a boy name ... Sister Mary Joseph. This meant that we were in the hands of an entirely new species.

On that very first day, Sister Mary Joseph wasted no time outlining the challenges that we urchins would be facing for the rest of our lives. She offered three questions:

> Where did you come from?
>
> Why are you here?
>
> Where are you going?

Pretty heavy stuff. We had no idea what she was talking about. Our interests were limited to things like sharpening new pencils and waiting impatiently for a recess so we could run around like the kids we really were. She explained the answers, again with that wonderful smile. They sounded OK, but involved new thoughts for basically untrained brains. Like good little angels, we listened, but without a clue that these questions would be following us around for the rest of our lives.

Now, more than three-quarters of a century later, these questions still sit there. Likely, they will never be fully answered, because we lack the capacity to wrap our logical minds around such esoteric or theological concepts. However, we can speculate about the answers to questions one and three dealing with origin and destiny because there is a gift called faith. This asset enables us to engage in such mysterious endeavors as placing faith in others, falling in love, and trust. Things that transcend physical evidence. Faith enables us to ponder and believe in where we came from and where we are going absent physical evidence. Matters of faith, by definition, defy definition.

Well, question two is where the fun starts. Why are we here? This one is not only easier but has teeth in it. We have our own everyday lives as report cards. We can grade our own performance and also plan our next actions. All under our own supervision. An important thing called accountability. Of course, Sister Mary Joseph wanted us to be aware that our existence should be high minded and in the service of a higher authority. That is reasonable and noble. Surely, she wanted us to be good all the time, but knew that even little angels would have their bad days. We would be on our own and learn these lessons in due course.

Sister Mary Joseph provided us with a beautiful canvas to paint our own portraits.

· Our Pandemic Heroes ·

The unwelcome pandemic lingered on.

There are so many stories that have taken place during this prolonged challenge. The impact on each and every person on this planet has been a story in itself. In stepping back and trying to feel the emotional nature of these stories, we find ourselves thinking about our heroes. People we've never met. Yes, we know them in our everyday lives. Seen, but not really appreciated. It is sad to admit that, in normal times, their roles were almost taken for granted. No one wants to be thought of in this light. We all believe that our lives have purpose and goals. It is unfortunate that it takes a crisis to appreciate just how important each human being can be. Our heroes. Especially the unsung kind.

The first group of heroes is our health care professionals. They have become so famous that they really morphed into headline heroes. And rightly so. It is impossible to discuss the topic of heroes without recognizing the outstanding contributions of our healthcare professionals. Our story begins with these special people. Their chosen mission in life is to help others who find themselves in distress. A noble starting point. A calling that operates 24 hours every day. Life threatening situations are nothing new ... until something like a pandemic strikes. Although well-trained for just about any contingency, the sheer intensity, size and complexity of this attack was another story. It's one thing to deal with challenges of long hours, overcrowding of facilities and understaffing. The list of obstacles was frightening. From the onset of this scourge, our heroes faced a shortage of equipment and supplies. Then, when you add in the mixed signals of administrators with the conflicting opinions of the so-called experts, you have a real-life crisis. The fickle nature of this new virus not only confounded scientists but resulted in an ever-changing game plan. Our heroes were caught in this whirlpool. Somehow, they prevailed. Their performance has not only touched our hearts but has taught us the lesson of fortitude. We love our healthcare angels and continue to marvel at their sustained efforts. They always come through. Our ongoing thanks will never catch up to their never-ending help.

Suddenly, hundreds of millions of us had to be protected and fed.

That brings us to our next group of heroes. These are our own neighbors who work in a segment of the economy known as the "service sector". Roughly, this means anyone who is engaged in providing services to the general public. These are people that know us very well. It is a huge category of jobs, largely comprised of people who have extensive experience dealing directly with customers. This means that they are in sync with our wide range of needs. This also means they are blessed with patience. People enter this field because they derive satisfaction from assisting other human beings. The pandemic landed on service sector jobs with a knockout punch. Essential services could only be delivered by people who were in a position to serve a population who are either confined to their own residences or limited in their in their travels. Our only links for survival. Oddly, we probably never thought about this barrel of services as life rafts. When lives are conducted in a business-as-usual fashion, it is understandable that we might even take many of these services for granted. With a pandemic, the world is turned upside down. Millions of us need help from our friends in the public service sector to survive in such a strange new world of dependency.

The tools of protection continue to be in the hands of existing emergency services such as police and firefighters. Normally and rightfully, we take these services for granted because they have a proven track record of being responsive. Their performance has been maintained at their normal high standards despite a rapid spread of the virus, sickness in their own ranks and a major increase in call volume. They have done a great job of dealing with a disease that arrived uninvited into our part of the world. They have managed to do so without a clear battle plan telling them how to combat such a menace. Heroes every day.

The other major tools of survival have become the tasks of food suppliers and people who keep equipment working. Failure in either of these necessities would mean defeat. Enter our other everyday heroes. You know who you are. You changed your whole lives around to keep us around. You have worked long and crazy hours, automatically making your efforts "above and beyond". Your ongoing sacrifices and determination will never be forgotten by us, and by you, as well. Don't ever forget your performance. It should be remembered as one of the most worthwhile times in your lives. You are truly our unsung heroes.

Cannot finish this story without one more thought. Another group continues to show notable grit.

Us.

Given the grim nature of this beast, we've done okay.

Not heroes, but maybe worthy of an honorable mention.

· Good Taste ·

This is not a discussion about food.

We're talking about the differing opinions that occur when separate human beings are observing the same object or subject. For instance, when walking into someone's home along with another person, chances are you will both have immediate opinions regarding the owner's taste. If you like what you see, this lucky homeowner is blessed with good taste. You may even feel comfortable enough to let the owner know just how wonderful they are. If you don't like what you see, you should just keep silent. While it may be tacky to even flirt with judging others, we know it happens every day and we should have the sense to treat it as a humorous foible.

At this point in our talk, you may be conducting an evaluation of your own taste and trying to determine whether it is good or bad taste. Don't worry. We all have good taste, as long as we can find someone else who agrees with us.

Let's talk about commercial management of taste. This is a sinful capitalist tool. The most obvious culprits are the fashion and home furnishing industries. They intentionally set out to manage our taste. They want to make you feel guilty for wearing last year's garments or even thinking about hanging on to that outdated sofa. How dare you. You must keep up with latest vogues, the latest taste. This practice of keeping you in the market used to be called planned obsolescence. At least that was an obvious ploy, letting products wear out more quickly, thereby bringing you back more frequently for replacements. While this practice still exists, it is definitely more honest than the continuous use of changing taste to shame us into purchasing their latest products.

It can be something as simple as the fashion world changing the "in" colors of clothing every year or the home decoration gurus modifying how your home should look. Please don't tell us that these are just "trends" and forces outside of their control. We get it. We're just neither educated nor sophisticated enough to grade the goods being displayed for our purchase.

While we are on the topic of trend setting, what about the music industry? Who sets the stage for new styles of music? What does good taste have to do with music? Who are these people? This little subject called "taste" has suddenly grown into a mess. There are just too many style/trend setters out there. Especially for anyone who has zero interest in keeping up with any of them.

The subject of taste, though, remains simple. Remember the rule we talked about ... you always have good taste if you can find someone who agrees with you. Oh, just thought of another human trait. When you discover these compatible souls, do you sometimes refer to them as being "well informed"? This is the ultimate acknowledgement of both good taste and intelligence.

Just hope you're right.

· L'Amour Pour L'Armoire ·

It's probably trite to want to talk about a piece of furniture. However, it's just possible that quite a few of us human beings become attached to one or more pieces of our furniture. Something like a favorite comfy sofa or an ancient dining room table. Innate objects that become part of the family. With us, it has been an armoire.

Back in our pioneer days in the late 1960s, we were attempting to convert an abandoned horse stable and groom's cottage into a house with two young children along for the ride. This was not a time for frills. Because this structure really had no closets for hanging clothes, we survived by everyone trying to manage their own modest collections of clothes. There came a time when this remedy became unwieldy, especially for the adults who had day jobs.

We decided to buy a stand-alone closet, something we had believed might work as a tentative solution. We went to a large store that had no definition. It was known as, "You know the place." Technically, it was a moving/storage operation, but it was known as a place where unwanted furniture could be purchased at bargain prices. Most of their unwanted inventory was relegated to the basement. Only selected items were placed out on the sidewalk where they could be displayed either for sale or ridicule. We decided to go down into the inner sanctum where we were told that we might find something close to what we were looking for. Luckily, we spotted a beauty that was buried deep in rows of similar sized pieces and therefore unseen by competing buyers. Our little gem. We managed to push aside other big pieces and decided to ask for a quote. With this enterprise, actual prices were secrets only to be shared with a select few. This is where the fun started. The owners were not only experts about furniture but were well-trained psychologists. The one-on-one haggling started. Firm but polite. A price was agreed upon and a sale was made. The owners of the establishment confirmed that this item was, indeed, an armoire. A piece of furniture that deserved to be placed in a bedroom that would henceforth be known as the "master" bedroom. A title that our children would certainly dispute.

Fast forward to the early 21st century. We had managed to move more than 12 times between 1968 and 2017. This meant that only a select portion of furniture would be able to tag along. However, the one-and-only piece of furniture that made it through to our final home was, guess what, the armoire. All the other stragglers were unceremoniously left behind. This relic somehow survived even the most arduous hurdles, including unbelievably awkward staircases. On more than one occasion, a canvas strap equivalent to a big rubber band was wrapped around the armoire to keep it from falling apart.

This brings us to the real motive for telling this story. Recently, we happened to be looking at our old friend and realized that it had little wheels attached. An unusual setup for an armoire. Also, there was a row of drawers next to the big closet door. Another anomaly. Obviously, these unusual features were something that we should have noticed over the years, but this piece of furniture was so efficient that we never paused to question its heritage. Armed with this curiosity, we searched Google. Surprisingly, we were referred to a piece of furniture called a CHIFFOROBE. This apparently is a smaller version of an armoire that was first introduced in the United States in 1908 via a Sears and Roebuck catalog. We actually owned a very special piece of Americana.

How about that? We spent all those years hanging on to a piece of furniture that we thought was imported and was almost like owning an antique. We should have known that something as delicate as an armoire was not suitable for such a rough journey. The chifforobe turned out to be the proper roughneck companion for our kind of adventures.

L'Amour pour l'Armoire no more. Welcome home chifforobe.

· Zappy Birthday ·

Thanks to hi-tech we can zap messages to anyone, anytime, anywhere. Especially around holidays like birthdays, anniversaries, and the like. Real timesavers. No fuss, no muss.

Whoops. What about grandma's or grandpa's birthday? From what we've heard, they really don't have many nice things to say about hi-tech. Should we decide to use this "with it" method of greeting, there's a very good chance that our thoughtful gestures will never be received by the grandparents. Sure, our clever device will tell us that they have received our message. Hah! Reality at the end of the transaction may tell another story. It may be buried in a sea of unsolicited messages, deleted by mistake, or simply never opened. There are just too many perils on the receiving ends of electronic wizardry. Especially with birthday greetings.

Ugh. The solution requires purchasing a greeting card. Do these things still exist? And, if so, where does one buy them? Hallmark stores? Here's the shocker ... greeting cards not only exist, but their sales are reaching historic levels. Even traditional card buyers are shocked by this phenomenon. They are seeing racks of cards, displayed everywhere. Supermarkets, drugstores, even hardware stores. All these outlets are even now starting to promote "deluxe" greeting cards at premium prices.

Why is this happening? It's arduous to stand there in those long racks of cards and try and pick out "just the right" one for the recipient. And then, the hardships of having to buy stamps (maybe even a packet of stamps), and finally, a postal location to mail this special gesture. Already, we are into a major expenditure of time and money. Is all this effort worthwhile?

It would be great to be there when they open their card.

We would have our answer.

· Labels ·

Do you like being labeled?

Ok, in the world of elections, we normally register in a particular party because, in many states, this is necessary to vote in the primaries. We engage in this practice despite the dilemma that it is increasingly difficult to get a handle on where the traditional parties stand. It is interesting to note that an impressive number of people are registering as "independents". This is good for a couple of reasons: it demonstrates a reluctance to identify with a party and creates a welcome dilemma for those annoying career political analysts who think that we are predictable.

However, this talk is not about traditional party labels. It's about a current phenomenon wherein groups of people are being arbitrarily thrown into categories invented by unknown sources. Where did all this stuff come from? It's a safe bet that the instigators of this activity are not happy people. It's also apparent that the media have played a key role in promoting these "labels". By repeating these labels over and over, they become part of the nomenclature. There's one slight problem with this type of thinking ... how does it work toward fixing grievances? Our destiny as a country will be determined by our ability to work together in good faith, not by labels which carry resentment. In such a world, there is no room for demonizing groups of others on the basis of fabricated inequities.

One final thought on this topic of herding people into categories ... their common denominator is the fact that they reek of negativity. Their messages take you on a one-way road to nowhere. Although we all should be offended by labels, their proliferation and lack of substance reminds us of the worth and sanctity of individuals. Here's a suggestion for a banner or tee shirt stating the one label that makes sense:

"I'M ONE OF A KIND"

We would all love to vote for someone we believe to be a person who makes realistic promises. It is encouraging to remember that there have been several presidents whose actions transcended labels. I'm sure you will recall some of their famous statements. They are signifigant, because they illustrate that individuals can rise above the constraints of labels or political orthodoxy.

"Ask not what your country can do for you - ask what you can do for your country"
"The Buck Stops Here"
"Mr. Gorbachev, tear down this wall!"
Let's abandon labels.
They just divide and diminish everyone.

· Our Unknown Hero ·

This is a story about heroism and someone we never knew.

What was the "Murmansk Run"? Most people remember that it had something to do with World War II. Well, it was the name adopted for a critical supply line to Russia that would provide materials to fend off a German invasion. Most historians agree that the success of this operation was one of the most important turning points in the conduct of that horrendous war. Germany had already overcome most European countries to the west and was threatening Great Britain. Their invasion of Russia was underway, hindered only by adverse weather conditions. If they defeated Russia, Great Britain would surely fall.

The allied forces determined that the only way to prevent this catastrophe was to immediately begin shoring up Russia's forces with additional weaponry and supplies. The only feasible route to Russia was via the sea. This meant that an unbroken chain of cargo ships had to be created, capable of sailing from a variety of ports up through the treacherous North Atlantic and Bering Sea. No such an amalgamation of ships was to be found. It had to be conceived, planned, and built. Right away. Failure to do so would mean disaster.

The plan called for recruiting every possible available cargo vessel, rounding up crews and immediately starting building, from scratch, a new fleet of cargo ships. This last piece of the puzzle included the Americans who agreed to build vessels known as "Liberty Ships". These extraordinary joint efforts produced enough ships and manpower to complete over 85 convoys to Russia, each consisting of an average of more than 50 cargo ships. These convoys sustained heavy losses both of ships and crews. The North Atlantic waters were laced with German warships, everything from submarines and destroyers to battleships. Add to the mix the infamously horrible weather of the North Atlantic where the sheer weight of ice forming on ships could cause them to sink. You have disasters as the norm. A place for only the brave.

Into this cauldron a group of unheralded men manned these cargo ships. They were serving as members of the Unites States Merchant Marines. They were civilians, a portion of whom were either underage or who had never been aboard a ship. It is difficult to picture these recruits caught in the cauldron of the North Atlantic infested with German submarines and destroyers. Imagine completing just one of these convoys and then doing it all over again. They sustained unbelievably heavy losses of life. These men were incredible.

We want to introduce you to a man that captained these cargo ships.

His name is Captain Thor Halverson.

In 1969 we purchased a house whose prior owner was Captain Halverson. He had passed away several years earlier and the property was therefore held in his estate. Lawyers involved in this matter were not personally acquainted with Captain Halverson but did mention that they understood he had been a sea captain. The property had been unoccupied for several years and was in a state of disrepair. In our preoccupation with the restoration, especially with two young children along for the ride, we failed to conduct any further research concerning the property. Over the years, however, we occasionally received additional information from neighborhood sources concerning the Halverson family, including these basic facts:

Captain Halverson served in World War II as captain of cargo ships in the Murmansk Run. His wife was a medical doctor and worked at a New York City hospital. They had one child, a girl, who died at an early age. Mrs. (Dr.) Halverson then died of cancer. After these tragedies, Captain Halverson became a recluse, and the property began to deteriorate. He passed away, isolated and alone.

While we had always been curious about the Halverson family and sympathized with their misfortunes, our primary concern was bringing this property back to life. It was not until seeing recent World War II documentaries on television and looking into the faces of those ninety-year-old heroes and sensing their sacrifices did we awaken to the magnitude of Captain Halverson's experiences. It made us think about Captain Halverson and his family. How many runs to Russia did he make? Did any of his ships get torpedoed and, if so, how was he and his crew rescued? How often did he get to be with his family? All of these questions, of course, have no probable answers unless we somehow are in touch with distant relatives or anyone who might be familiar with Captain Halverson's history.

This brings us to our motivations for writing this story. First and foremost is to pay a tribute to this man. He must have been an unbelievably strong and determined person to have lived through such an ordeal. Second, to applaud the services of his fellow merchant mariners who have never received proper recognition for their sacrifices. And, last, to harbor the slim hope that our little story may somehow reach some individuals or family members who may have further information regarding this very special man.

Thank you, Captain Halverson.

Our unknown hero.

· Mutiny Without Bounty ·

Some of us are constantly criticized for using too much Bounty. Sorry, but that's our calling. We all must do our part to keep this product around. There would be no life without Bounty.

Need proof? The Pandemic. Which paper towel sold out right away? Which shelves were empty for the longest annoying stretch? And, to add insult to this shortage, what pathetic products tried to fill this void? Please. It was like asking minor league ballplayers to bat for Babe Ruth. These pathetic substitutes would disintegrate at the sight of any little spill.

Bounty does every task thoroughly and efficiently, enabling everyone to lead a normal life. Otherwise, we would drown in a sea of spilled liquids. Our countertops would be encrusted with layers of crud and eventually decay. Mountains of dust would gather everywhere. Windows would become cloudy openings. Although once-upon-a-time there used to be things called "rags", these were merely little pieces of rejected materials that were neither designed nor qualified for this type of work. These rags just pushed dirt around and, to boot, the job of washing these little pieces of cloth was both time consuming and endless. When Bounty arrived on the scene, we were skeptical. How could big rolls of paper possibly save our lives? They called this product a "paper towel". How bold and pretentious!

The thought of paying good money for worthless rolls of paper was both an insult to our work ethic and an admission of defeat. Then, the geniuses at Proctor and Gamble gambled and used a well-known actress in their TV commercials to provide comfort and assurance. Nancy Walker. One of Us. A scrappy, hardnosed, down-to-earth personality. If Nancy believed that these rolls of paper were heaven sent, it was time to give them a try. She guaranteed that they were the "quicker-picker-uppers", and who wouldn't believe Nancy? This marketing strategy paid off, and Bounty gained immediate credibility. Everyone experimented and confirmed that, finally, here was a product that actually worked as promised. This universal acceptance was historic because it took place in an era when TV ads promoted flimsy products and gimmicks that rarely proved to be anything but "as advertised".

Bounty settled in. It even became a common noun. We dropped the phrase "paper towel" and inserted Bounty in its place. This is the ultimate dream of any business. Historically, there have been other examples where this phenomenon has taken place. Xerox and Kleenex come to mind. These namesakes enjoyed a burst of acceptance. However, because similar products were either improved or became so plentiful, these "pioneer" names gradually faded away. Not so with Bounty. If anything, it is more entrenched than ever. Being prom queen and class valedictorian at the same time can be heady stuff. Will P&G become complacent or piggy?

We think not. They did, however, boldly introduce a new version called "SELECT-A-SIZE". They actually decided to offer this beloved product in sheets that were one half the size of the well-known full size. Traditionalists were horrified. How could they! Well, this gamble worked out just fine. It turns out that their product is so effective that even smaller sizes get the job done. This also satisfied the more frugal customers who had watched certain members of their household carelessly use full-sized sheets on the teeniest spills. Another gamble. Another win.

It's refreshing to know that quality is still alive today.

Without Bounty, there would be a mutiny.

· Coulda, Woulda, Shoulda ·

These three little slang words always seem to be coupled together, maybe trying to give them an illusion of strength. Ironically, their togetherness just emphasizes their whimsical nature. Offered in humor, sometimes taking responsibility for missed opportunities, but seeming to blame outside forces. We listen, knowing full well that we also have a basket full of these feelings. It is human nature to carry around the memory of events that didn't work out as planned.

However, take heart ... here are a few slang words that are positive. Try "wanna" and "gonna" on for size. These immediately introduce the element of control. They both deal with the future, not the irretrievable past."Wanna" is a wish, but not a crazy unreachable one. For example, when someone says, "I wanna go skiing in Colorado next year," we know that this is a dreamy wish, but full of good intentions. All in all, "wanna" has energy and credibility. Tolerance for listening to "wannas" depends on our patience in listening to individuals who may have a tendency to make too many wishes.

The big winner in our slang contest is "gonna". It even sounds guttural. It is true that some individuals may abuse this wonderful word by making too many promises. Please ignore them. Also, we might want to evaluate casual promises that are unlikely to be fulfilled. When "gonna" is spoken with conviction it carries a degree of credibility that slang words generally do not enjoy.

Whoops ... just thought of another slang saying that many of us use too frequently. With me, when my favorite football or baseball team is consistently playing poorly, I find myself muttering over and over ... "YAGOTTA BELIEVE!!"

It never works.

· Brains ·

I've been thinking about donating my brain to science. Installed over eighty years ago and hardly ever used. For sure, no organ has ever been donated in such a pristine condition.

I also thought about donating my gut, which houses my instinctive powers. This mysterious mechanism would likely be of no interest to science. Mainly, because it is worn out, having carried the load that should have been handled by my brain. Also, why in the world would scientists be interested in a mechanism that actually arrives at practical solutions. Scientists only like to follow science, which is really whatever they decide. Especially in teams.

These days, we are finding ourselves relying more frequently on instinct. This is due to frustration. Human beings are encountering things that are either nonsensical or intentionally misleading. Our only reliable option is to use our trusted experience, logic and common sense. Instead of sitting around and moping about problems, we must turn on the instinct switch. A light goes on. We don't really know if this is exactly the answer we want, but we definitely feel comfortable. This comfort level is important ... not only because it is based upon both our very own knowledge and conscience, but it rules out acceptance of conclusions that have been presented by unknown or untrustworthy sources.

Brains make lousy donor gifts. Too rigid. Too opinionated.

Instincts would be wonderful gifts.

They work.

· The Golf Panacea ·

The game of golf can help make you a better person.

Forget traditional golf lessons. They deal with grips, stances and the type of minutiae that freeze your brain and clogs the highway of nerves running from your head down to your moving parts. Instead, let "big picture" thoughts seep into those same brain cells that shut down over a three-foot putt. Just relax. Lessons learned from this little story will enable you to have a deeper understanding regarding the reasons for your attraction to a game that, to the casual observer, appears to be played with primitive tools on big, pretty lawns. Golf affords you the rare gift of learning more about yourself as a person. This simple process will kick start your thinking and give you a new perspective on life.

The first thing you should know is the fact that golf is a game, not a sport. You don't engage in physical combat with an opponent like any normal sport. You are actually going into battle with a contrived piece of real estate. Ok, there are win/lose outcomes, but these results are based upon your ability to reduce the real estate to a whimpering piece of earth. It is always nice, though, to score better than the other human beings who happen to be present at the time.

Now, let's dissect the game, and how it makes you a better person.

First, there's this thing called preparation. You know, the skill that makes lawyers and bartenders so professional. The prep stage involves such challenges as time management (carving 5 to 7 hours out of your to-do list), budgeting (dipping into earmarked dollars), scheduling (coordinating with golf partners, arranging tee times, and then frequently changing all of these), updating inventory (dealing with outdated equipment and golf outfits) and a host of other challenges that are designed to test your readiness and reconfigure your brain to start a game that has absolutely no bearing on your "other" life... the one with all those responsibilities.

Next, comes actually playing the game. Remember, your enemy is the piece of real estate, not the people you have elected to spend time with. Like life itself, starting out with a positive thought process should end up with positive results. Trouble is, your golf game could disrupt your equilibrium right away, starting off badly with a stinker on your first shot on the very first hole. You immediately learn how to deal with adversity. What a game! You've just started, and you are already dealing with problem solving. Character building starts early.

Once underway, the game takes on a non-stop barrage of challenges. You are facing the prospect of adverse weather, poor course conditions, mental breakdowns, and errant shots. And, to add to the fun, those evil course designers have strategically located a host of mean-spirited hazards, such as sand traps, ponds and big trees, all placed in nasty locations. Now, once you have worked your way through these impediments, you arrive at a place called a "green". You are now being asked to deal with slick grass that grows on an undulating surface. Here, you are required to make the difficult adjustment of your golf swing from a robust effort to a gentle, caring stroke. This entails striking the golf ball with a small stick that has the funny name of "putter". It is a stick that looks nothing like your other sticks and is responsible for sending the dimpled ball into a very small hole. Success in this part of the game not only is a disproportionate share of your final score, but may impact your continued interest in playing the game. The big irony is the simple fact that these little strokes become more important when the distances you must advance the ball become shorter and shorter. The shorter the distance, the greater the chances of having your brain lock down. Mental health versus brute strength. Guess who wins.

What we have just experienced together is a summary of what occurs when you try to match up athletic ability with mental stability, all happening on just one golf hole, repeated 18 times. Who would play such a game?

Here's the truth:

Golfers play the game to test themselves. It's not only about skill and challenges. It also involves integrity. Golf is one of the rare games where players not only keep their own score, but also must adhere to numerous stringent rules of golf. This honesty takes place throughout, even when a player may be out of sight of other golfers. As an example of this special trait, in situations where the ball lands in an unfortunate location, a player "must hit the ball where it lies". This is the equivalent of the real-life principle, "Play the cards you are dealt." All of these constraints and rules have the effect of placing responsibility directly on the shoulders of each golfer. It reinforces the need for accountability in one's life. All good.

Oh, almost forgot. We've talked about how preparation, handling adversity, and integrity can make you a better person. How do these builders of character also make you a better golfer? That's easy… a confident well-adjusted person brings relaxation to the contest, and, in golf, this translates into smooth, effortless motion, the elixir of a great golf swing.

Relax. Have fun.

And bring along your sense of humor.

· Foibles ·

Don't worry, we'll never be perfect. We were first exposed to perfection in grade school where we ran into our very first teacher's pets. These were little angels who always handed in perfect papers. These submissions not only had 100% correct answers, but were meticulously packaged, with perfectly aligned punch holes and a sturdy cover. Teachers compounded this unfortunate situation by holding these perfect works up high and suggesting to the rest of us slugs that this was the way we should perform for the rest of our lives. This little lecture never worked. None of us liked these teacher's pets. As a matter of fact, we probably decided right then and there to never be like these exemplary little angels.

Well, we didn't have to worry. We would never be perfect. A thing called foibles would always bring us back to reality. It is such a pervasive trait, that it may even disrupt teacher's pets as they proceed through life. Just try and imagine such an event. The perfectionist stumbles, revealing the fallacy of perfection and the truth of humanity. Luckily, most of us had already started experiencing this reality, maybe even as early as grade school.

Foibles are good. Sometimes they arrive as a surprise. How many times have we repeated to ourselves, "How stupid am I!" or, "I don't believe I did that!" Foibles are nothing more or less than mistakes. The tricky part is keeping them in perspective. If you find yourself encountering more foibles than your fair share, maybe it's time to look at perspective. This will involve shedding some of the trivial items.

Tough love. The hard business of concentrating on stuff that matters.

· Penny and Charlie ·

For most human beings, it takes a lifetime to figure things out. Even then, maybe never. Luckily, we have critters amongst us who apparently have the answers. Perhaps, the best example is dogs. OK, we realize that cats are smart. Maybe too smart. Dogs are decidedly more like us. Anxious to please, but capable of walking into walls. Dogs have sappy smiles. No, correct that ... technically, their lips don't turn up. However, we know that they are smiling because we see it in their eyes and telltale tail-wagging. These reactions are triggered by visions and brain cells that sense good things are happening. Although their rear-ends are the most obvious evidence, we always perceive them as happy, smiling critters.

Let's start using our dogs as our role models. Keep it simple. Just observe their behavior. Pretend you want to be like them. Luckily, we have Penny and Charlie as our teachers, with their faces as our textbooks. They tell us …

Be joyous of life …
Love everyone, no matter the breed …
Jump over every hurdle …
Comfort one another …
Dress simply. . .
Always play well with others.

· Just in Time ·

Artificial Intelligence to the rescue! As senior citizens, we have been dealing with how to improve both the capacity and accuracy of our aging brains. Finally, we can relax.

Just start pushing some buttons on the device of our choosing. How considerate, how understanding, how simple. If you want progress, you are required to be progressive and open-minded. However, please be warned that this could be a treacherous playing field for seniors. Our not so nimble fingers find their way along on these little keys while also dreading the possibility of deletions. Despite all these dangers and complete lack of training, we venture forward. We didn't get this far in life by being whussies.

Some of us like to write stories. Pick one of your favorites and turn on the magic wand. Based upon the hoopla, it seems that all we would have to do is enter a few nouns and pronouns, and then sprinkle in some verbs along with adverbs, whatever they are. A proposed plot would help, along with some characters. But let's not get ahead of ourselves. The whole idea is to have AI do all the work. Let's just start with a simple scenario. All senior citizens have huge storerooms of memories. Most of these just sit there, patiently waiting for their turn to be remembered. However, quite a few seem to be cropping up either regularly or emphatically. These special memories cry out to be told.

As an example, our family would love to write a story about our working together attempting to convert an abandoned building into living quarters while simultaneously living inside this structure. We could even provide a few grainy pictures of this adventure. And should AI find itself lost or confused; we would be happy to include a few funny anecdotes as comic relief. Because all of us will be working together in a new experiment, we should clarify our roles. We see ourselves as consultants. There to help but trusting AI to control the ballgame and carry us to a touchdown. Don't get us wrong ... we love to work with others. It's just that we've never worked before with an electronic brain. It would be a nice gesture of the geniuses behind this invention to come up with a user-friendly name for our new co-worker. Something like "smarty pants" would be OK. Also, we know it's old-fashioned to ask, but it would be nice to see a few drafts of our proposed story.

It may be presumptuous believing that our input might be helpful, but we understand that AI is in its infancy and might not be ready for gushy, emotional stories. All we can do is offer to participate in this grand experiment. Please tell us what to do next.

You arrived just in time!

· Caring ·

As much as we might want to, we just can't stop caring. Even Rhett Butler when he shouted at Scarlett O'Hara "I don't give a damn!", he really didn't mean it. He cared immensely about having his life turned upside down and losing the love of his life. His anger was caring personified. Try it yourself, muttering I don't care, or I don't give a damn. All we are doing is affirming that we, in fact, do care.

Now that we have established that it is impossible to bury this emotion, maybe it's a good idea to think about how we might possibly take another look at caring. We might even explore suggestions containing practical applications of this powerful emotion. Let's start by identifying the things we care about. The idea is to weed the garden. Throw out, or at least tone down, the piggy ones. Next should be those troubling survival items like finances. Ok, we know that staying afloat is a vital concern, but worrying too much about money can turn into fretting. Let's not fret. To do so raises the possibility of introducing fear, a well-known enemy of caring. That leaves us with the obvious categories of personal matters that we treasure such as families, religious beliefs, friendships, neighbors, and all those familiar situations where caring is a vital and active force. Nurture these.

What about all the leftover caring? In our daily lives, we become aware of situations where our fellow human beings find themselves in need. These observations are always emotional and prompt feelings of guilt that we are not doing anything to help unfortunate souls. One option is to locally volunteer our time and/or financial support for a specific organization. Another great alternative is to electronically authorize regular monthly payments to reputable organizations whose work has proven to be effective and well-managed. All good.

Caring is such a beautiful thing. It's nice that we can spread it around.

· Comfortable ·

How about this great word! Its meaning and substance never change. As a matter of fact, as civilization meanders out of control, the word comfortable has become more essential than ever. The more the chaos, the greater need to feel comfortable.

Most words have an antonym. Sometimes, this opposite meaning can even be stronger than the primary word. Clearly, comfortable wins this battle. The opposing uncomfortable may be capable of introducing elements of concern, but these temporary doubts lack conviction. It is entirely natural to have misgivings when entertaining any decisions that matter. To illustrate this phenomenon, I am going to provide a bit of insight that went into my thinking when I decided to attempt writing at such a seemingly late stage of life.

I struggled with making decisions. Who was I to express my thoughts and opinions on any topic? How could I dare to pretend to know anything about anything. My only credentials were based upon real life experiences and observations. In this contemplative mode, there was a point reached where I felt uncomfortable. What was the downside? Strangers would be thinking … who in the world is this guy … he doesn't even seem to have any expertise. Well, too bad. All of us have a perfect right to express our feelings and beliefs. Given this green flag, words started to spill out and my confidence level seemed to grow. I became grounded, convinced that anyone who would take the time to read and ponder these words may at least appreciate their honesty. Trying to gain agreement from anyone has never been an objective. Quite the opposite is true. I want to learn.

Once I understood that readers were to be trusted and certainly would be honest critics, I reached the lofty status of feeling comfortable. I really can't give you a better example of how this wonderful phenomenon miraculously manages to create peace of mind.

Yes, I am comfortable with you.

Part II

Real-life Stories

· Worst Case Scenario: Our First House ·

Most first-time house buyers are mentally and financially unqualified to engage in such an endeavor. Clueless is a word that comes to mind. Our story is true. If you are an apartment dweller or a smug first-time homeowner in denial who only remembers your purchase as a trouble free experience, you probably should not venture into our world.

The decision to move out of our beloved New York City was made for the familiar reasons of affordability and two young children, plus a Labrador retriever. This simple, reasonable decision was screwed up from the get-go, as we set our targeted home location to be a village in a suburban area that was completely out of our price range. According to real estate experts, this is a common mistake that spells big trouble ahead. Deep down, we must have realized that this was a stupid way to begin our mission. However, as we learned once the adventure began, we always reached for the unreachable ... You'll see.

Our story takes place in the late 1960's. It was a simpler time without gadgets like web browsing, cell phones or other devices to help us weave through the minefield of options. We had to tough it out the old-fashioned way ... from start to finish in the hands of a local real estate agency. We don't mean that real estate agents are bad people. Quite the opposite. It's just that we were scared to death that our big desires and little budget would get lost in a busy suburban office. Well, we traveled by subway and Metro North to our selected utopian village and walked to the nearest real estate office. It looked like a business that catered to wealthy clients, with subdued signage and a pair of potted evergreens standing sentry at the doorway. There were no photos of houses scotch taped to the store windows. A classy place. We stepped into the reception area, awaiting a greeting. Nothing happened. We looked around and noted that the office was occupied solely with women, all of whom wore tailored outfits and appeared to have much more money than we had or would ever have.

It was obvious that we were being sized up as young prospects. We were in an age group that is infamous for lack of money and real-world education. We wondered how they would decide who the lucky agent would be assigned to help us ... a rookie? ... someone who screwed up a recent deal? As it turned out we were greeted by an individual who appeared to be both seasoned and professional. To protect her fine reputation in the industry as a seller of high-end realty, we are using the pseudonym "Blanche" to identify this nice person. Apparently, Blanche was just finishing up a huge sales year and was anxious to take on a prospect that would be less stressful than her million-dollar deals. Also, she had children that were about our age and was comfortable dealing with dysfunctional young adults.

As we outlined our impossible goals, i.e. nice house, best neighborhood, low price, etc., Blanche quietly took notes. Her first remark was a gentle suggestion that the market might be a tad too high for our dream house. She was careful not to paint a bleak picture because discouraging talk is forbidden in the real estate sales handbook. She explained that due to the fact that there were no descriptions and pictures of properties in our price range included in the Agency's glossy brochure, we had to resort to a guided tour. It was kind of like blind dates ... each prospect had a nice personality but had to be sized up on their own appearance. We climbed into Blanche's late model luxury vehicle, a Cadillac convertible with leather interior. A nice ride. What we saw on that tour was a real-world revelation. If there was an internet available in the 1960s, the properties we saw from the car would have been listed on their website as "The 10 Most Unwanted Houses". If they were horses in a sweepstakes race, they would have been "also rans". We never got out of the car for a closer inspection. We got the picture. We were out of our league.

Blanche was not discouraged. Not one little bit. She must have had an ace up her sleeve. We wondered if this was a proven real estate technique: show a bunch of shacks and soften up the clients with a dose of reality. It certainly worked for us. She had sized us up as having limited finances, but also possessing an underlying streak of non-conformity. She was about to test her powers of observation. She drove into a fancy neighborhood, and we politely asked her if she was lost. This was a stupid question. Professional real estate people are never lost. And then, suddenly, she turned down the paved driveway that appeared to belong to a very substantial home. Further in, it turned into a muddy track that was more typical of an ATV trail somewhere in the wilderness. The Cadillac came to a stop. We peeked through the car windows and saw what looked like a building, almost hidden among overgrown vines, trees and bushes.

This was it!

Before we even got out of the car, a gut decision had flashed through our beings. This type of emotional reaction is known to completely shut down the brain and stop all rational thinking. We fell in love with our first home while still sitting in the Cadillac. Our brains were locked and loaded before we even stepped out of the car. We then cautiously walked towards the building, which looked like a barn or garage. Around the back, there was an attached structure that appeared to be a small house. As it turned out, the main structure was actually a stable and the attachment was a "groom's cottage". We looked at each other and mumbled "groom's cottage?" being a type of housing we had never encountered. Throughout our story we will be referring to the complex as the "barn", a term of endearment we adopted for our new home.

Everything was boarded up as it had not been occupied for several years. We were told that teenagers liked to use the place for whatever was on their agenda. Fine. The exterior was painted a prison grey, peeling everywhere due to rotting siding. The most interesting feature of the roof was the large nest of some large unknown flying creature who undoubtedly would object to our cohabitation. The shingles were busy losing whatever asphalt remained on their surface. There was an interesting curvature to the top line of the roof, looking like the back of a swayback horse, mimicking the stable's former residents. We toured around the back of the buildings and discovered that we had neighbors ... a cemetery that was completely overgrown, but with a few old headstones peeking out through the vines and weeds. As you couldn't ask for quieter neighbors, we chalked this up as a bonus and buffer zone from other nearby homes. This was our preliminary take on the exterior of our future home. The best stuff awaited us inside.

Somehow, Blanche found an entry into the stable section. We were greeted by a dirt floor throughout. It was one large, open space with barn doors facing south and a garage door facing east. We envisioned four or five horses sharing space with a 1950's automobile, maybe a Gran Torino! There were four nicely preserved hand painted signs with horses' names proudly hung on opposing walls. The place smelled of hay, without much aroma from the horses. They probably moved out years ago. There were two doorways, one to the rear yard and one which had several steps up into the groom's cottage. Blanche advised us that the last owner of the property was a retired sea captain. He was actually a real-life hero, having survived many dangerous journeys in the North Atlantic Ocean during World War II. This was the infamous "Murmansk Run" to Russia where ships sustained heavy losses from German submarines. He was married to a physician who was an attending doctor at New York Hospital. How many women were physicians in the 1940s? We were in awe of both of their accomplishments. Understanding that a sea captain was involved with the house also helped to explain why the cottage was several feet higher that the stable. As we learned a few years later, there was a tidal basin nearby that had a tendency to flood the property during a severe Northeaster. During these storms the higher groom's cottage stayed above the highest floodwaters, the stable section was always in play and the basement took in water like the hole in the Titanic.

We resumed our tour at the higher-level groom's cottage. We entered what appeared to be the kitchen, an educated guess, as there was a rusted old sink and an equally rusted refrigerator.. We thought of the fridge as a unique "welcome wagon" gift, greeting the lucky new owners with an appliance that normally goes with a home sale. The kitchen floor was ugly linoleum, glued down, of course. There was a flu for some type of stove, probably coal burning. At this point we thought it was important to look at the basement. After all, this is normally where the heating source is located, or a game room or at least a tool room. There was a doorway in the kitchen that contained a rickety stairway down. We slowly crept down and discovered disappointment on all these assumptions. There was a metal hulk that must have been, at one point in time, a furnace of sorts. The broken cement floor was covered with water and there was a nook where lumps of wet coal were laying dormant. The metal hulk was therefore a coal furnace. We left the basement immediately, making certain this revelation would not impact on our firm decision to buy the place. When you are in denial about what you really see with your eyes, it's better to move along quickly.

We went back up the cellar stairs to the kitchen where a doorway led to the living room which had a small fireplace and some trashed furniture. There was a door to a very small porch, this presumably being the main entrance. A huge pine tree hovered over the porch, causing severe damage to both the porch and the house. The ceilings in the kitchen and living room were very low, ruling out ownership for any buyers over six feet. Luckily, we just made the limit, but wondered if our kids, with some ancestors who were quite tall, would be able to live here beyond their teens. Hmmm. There was a narrow stairway to the second floor. We all trooped up there, not knowing what to expect. At the top of the stairs was a small room, easily identified as a bathroom. It had an old toilet, a small sink and a relic claw-footed bathtub, all resting on the expected glued down linoleum. There were two other small rooms on the groom's cottage second floor, presumably bedrooms. They also had low ceilings and there was a strange absence of any closets. We then ventured though a doorway which opened into the second floor of the stable, a space that we decided was the hayloft. It looked like there was enough space to build two bedrooms and another bathroom. We carefully avoided the topics of when we would take on these projects or how we would begin to pay for them. This was no time for practical thinking … we had made an iron-clad decision to buy this so-called house. The interior walk-through can best be described as a trip through a structure that had been totally destroyed by neglect, floods, vandalism, animal infestation or any combination thereof.

We loved it!

Besides, we were looking forward to touring the actual property, our half acre of heaven. Blanche accompanied us on this exploration. It was tough to get our bearings as the entire property was overgrown with vines and fallen trees. As we ventured through the rough terrain, we noticed that the ground was very wet, and water was soon covering our shoes. Blanche finally had a topic she could address and said, "Oh, there's a swampy area ahead, but there is a plug you can pull out and the water will go away." This simple statement had to be one of the greatest real estate stories ever told. Our reaction was predictable, as we envisioned an old-fashioned white bathtub with one of those rubber plugs attached to a chain. Easy. Pull the plug … no swamp. Not a problem.

Even after these initial observations, our gut driven decision remained firm. The little problems like no water, no heat, no electricity, except through frayed wires, and finally, a swamp in the front yard were completely blocked from the rational sides of our brains. Our two liberal arts diplomas stapled together totaled zero practical knowledge of home ownership or construction. Nothing in our walk though had set off alarms. If we saw something scary, the phrase "no problem" was blurted out with the power of a super placebo. And, after all, the swamp did come with a nice big plug.

Where do we sign? Well, the property was in an estate, making things a little more adventurous. A sealed final bid would be necessary. This presented our first tactical dilemma … how do you estimate the value of a property that had no comparable home prices either in the area or the entire universe? The hackneyed phrase "one of a kind", for once, was right on. We elected to bid using the same strategy employed on our yearly trip to the racetrack, just pull a number out of the air. We bid $35,500. We won, beating some other wild and crazy bidder by $500. The next hurdle was coming up with earnest money (deposit), which we didn't have. We scrounged around among relatives and acquaintances, just making a one third down payment. Working with a local bank on a mortgage for the balance is, in itself, another story. Rather than have you speculate, we'll tell you right now that the loan must have been secured based upon our good looks and enthusiasm. They did perform a casual inspection of the house, insisting that that we at least paint the place and put up gutters on the roof. When they came back to see our progress the gutters were up, but we had managed to paint only two sides of the buildings. The gentleman from the bank was in a hurry, and we convinced him not to bother looking at the rear, or unpainted, part. Luckily, he left after viewing only two sides of the house. This was kind of a forerunner of the reckless Fannie Mae days, the only difference being our stubborn streaks that resulted in paying off the bank and other loans in full. However, this is not a story about money. The adventure that awaited us turned out to be so pure and unbelievable that it would be in bad taste to discuss monetary matters. Let's just say that we tackled the project one challenge at a time, blocking out the money pit considerations. The term "cost overruns" had no place in such a high-minded undertaking.

It was summertime, with the formal closing scheduled for late fall. The Estate took pity on us and permitted us to work on the property until the closing. While this sounds nutty, they must have rationalized that this nice young couple couldn't do any more damage than vandals and mother nature had already wrought. We tackled the challenge with mindless energy, cleaning and attempting to create a silk purse in record time. This hiatus was known as our rudimentary pioneer stage, similar to our 19th century forerunners who crossed the country and the Rockies in their Conestoga wagons. All cooking was performed on a single hot plate. The only water was a line that ended at the stable. It was our source for all cleaning chores, including ourselves as we set up a shower with a hose while standing on a piece of plywood. The one toilet was made functional by carrying a pail of water upstairs, dropping the water into the tank. It worked just fine, although we had no idea where the contents ended up.

During this period, the enormity of our task came into clearer focus. Where do we start? What about the kids? School was due to start. Winter was soon to follow. How do we heat the place? We had no answers. It was time to seek professional help to get us through this next critical stage. This would be our first encounter with reality ... working with complete strangers and about conveying our needs that, unfortunately, they would neither understand nor comply with. In order of urgency, plumbers and electricians shared the top spot. We started with a plumber, relying on the Yellow Pages. Our selection showed up a week later, slowly creeping down our muddy driveway in his clean late-model luxury foreign automobile. He disembarked, with a big smile. His annuity awaited, a lifetime of work envisioned, performed at the request of novices. Perfect. We outlined our basic plumbing needs. He kept repeating the phrase "no problem". Funny how he kept shrugging off what we saw as disasters. We never saw this gentleman again. He delegated this job to his workers. They proceeded to take the phrase "roughing in" to a new level in the plumbing industry. They drilled and chopped through several support structures, installing pipes wherever they thought was the shortest distance between two points. Their work was a key enlightenment for us. If the boss could drive a luxury auto, not show up, and still provide shoddy work, we were now going to change our method of operation. We would learn skills, and when we did get into situations over our heads, we would only engage "hands on" professionals who actually did the work. The next looming crisis was heating the groom's cottage, including the kids' bedrooms and, if there was any money left, also heating the hayloft area where we were planning to sleep. We don't want to keep you in suspense, so we're telling you now that our designated sleeping area was not heated for the next three years.

As city dwellers used to banging on radiators to have the superintendent send up some heat, the task of actually heating an entire building was beyond our universe. Several heating companies came and looked at our unique situation and while they initially salivated at the prospect of tackling a bare bones building, they sadly advised that getting fuel to our property was virtually impossible. There were no natural gas lines in the area, so fuel, whether oil or propane, had to be delivered by truck. We had jokingly been referring to our property in golfing terms as an "unplayable lie" due to the muddy, hilly driveway, the swamp and the overgrown vegetation. It seems that these oil companies agreed, and they were unwilling to risk having their expensive fuel trucks navigate this terrain, especially during the winter. As resuscitating the dead coal furnace was not viable, our only remaining option was electric heat. Surprisingly, during this particular time frame, they had special rates for residential usage. The cost differential versus fuel remained fairly stable until the mid 1970's when it became outrageous. To deal with this crisis, we installed a small coal burning stove in the kitchen. It turned out to be one of our rare smart moves ... it was a yummy kind of heat and almost heated every room in the groom's cottage all by itself.

So, we had partial heat and incomplete plumbing to settle in for the winter. Although our day jobs kept interfering, in our eyes, the place was becoming comfortable. However, it was stlll an absurd project in the view of first-time visitors. To measure this period of minimal improvements we had the observations of a number of curiosity seekers who looked in on us from time to time. On one such occasion, we had friends and their two children over for a visit. We were all sitting out on the teeny front porch. The parents were being totally kind and cautious with their observations saying things like "great potential", "charming", etc. We accepted their compliments with equal grace knowing full well that all of us were being disingenuous. One of their children wasn't so diplomatic … he moved next to his mother and asked, "Are they actually going to live in this dump?" We all heard this, and it helped clear the air. Our friends knew that we were unconventional and stubborn all in one package and that we would somehow survive. This was a healthy reminder that, like mothers everywhere, we had a house that only we could love.

You now are familiar with our starting point, so in order to condense the ensuing adventure into a readable short story, we are going to just highlight some of the events and mishaps that have been seared into our brains as being the most egregious and humorous. Keep in mind that we never kept notes or took a lot of pictures. We owned the house for twenty-four years, and due to changes in our lives, rented the place for the last twelve years of ownership. The period from disaster to rentable status was therefore about twelve years. This may seem like a long period of time for those people who are accustomed to quick turnarounds with rehab projects. However, we were slowed down by both a lack of funds and our own mistakes. Besides, we were having the best time of our lives. The major projects ahead that involved the interior were heating the stable and hayloft, building two new bedrooms and bathrooms, gutting and installing an updated kitchen and designing and creating a new entranceway with a guest half-bath, building a grand stairway to the second floor, installing new flooring throughout the stable and, lastly, building a new living room with picture windows overlooking the property. This was the condensed list for the interior. The exterior list consisted of fewer items which, nevertheless, were no picnic. Included were sanding and painting the entire building, including replacement of rotted siding, installing a new roof, paving the muddy driveway, clearing the overgrown vegetation everywhere and, finally, dealing with the swamp and creating a large pond. Oh, we almost forgot the septic system which was a trial-and-error event. One failed attempt followed by an expensive final fix. As you may have noticed, this was an impressive list. We lucked out with a creative architect and a reputable local construction company on the major items. We did all of the demolition work and some of the basic framing and sheetrocking on jobs like the upstairs bedrooms and bath. We also did the sanding and painting of the exterior along with all of the tile work in bathrooms and the kitchen. But our real expertise was all of the down and dirty items that required grunt labor. This included stuff that was not listed as major projects, like cleaning out all the rotted coal and gunk in the basement and dismantling and disposing of the relic coal furnace.

Pest control was also our specialty. As expected, an uninhabited and uncared for building had become a very attractive primary residence for rodents both big and small, squirrels, raccoons and an occasional skunk. The larger species of rodents were especially unwelcome. On one occasion, we baked a pecan pie and foolishly left it out on top of the refrigerator. They apparently loved pecans, eating these morsels off of the outside circle, but leaving their footprints in the center of the pie. Our other major residents, the squirrels, made their homes mostly in the attic where they slept during the day and partied every night. These party animals required full scale warfare. Their primary means of access was through rotted eaves and sofits along the edges of the roof. Due to the fact that this was an early problem prior to the major job of replacing the entire roof, it became our project. We rented scaffolding and ripped out about four feet of roof edges, rebuilding a solid barrier to keep these critters out for good. We were really proud of our effort and workmanship. Only we forgot several things ... were there any squirrels left in the house, and were they now trapped as permanent residents? Do they have a means of escape? There were no good answers. In a moment of inspiration, we decided to build a squirrel-sized gangway, a narrow board running from the attic area to a small opening in a window. We sprinkled talcum powder (Shower to Shower) on the gangway, providing us with evidence of their escape. The fact that they might use this as an entryway didn't really phase us, as we would see the direction of their footprints in the Shower-to-Shower talcum powder. Brilliant. Except it didn't work. We saw no evidence of movement, in or out. However, a few days later, one solitary squirrel showed up inside the small coal stove in the kitchen, making one hellish racket. It was summertime, so our guest was not dancing on hot coals. How he/she got there, probably through the stove's flu up on the roof, was not a big deal. How to remove it was. Squirrels get very squirrelly when trapped. Our brilliant son had the solution: we merely carried the stove with the squirrel inside to the back of the property… we opened the stove door, and the critter returned to the wild, free to continue its efforts to re-enter the house.

The interior work performed over the twelve-year period was fairly conventional, with no major surprises or setbacks. The exterior work was, itself, a lifetime project. Especially the swamp. The famous bathtub type plug was not to be found; no doubt due to our inept search. The fact that a good deal of the property was under water, and possibly below sea level, intrigued not only us, but just about everyone who saw the phenomenon. One of our early local contractors was enamored with the prospect of creating a pond with his very own backhoe. There was one slight problem. His backhoe was not up to the job. After a few hours of hearing his diesel motor object to the torture of working in mud halfway up the height of the backhoe's wheels, he disembarked and said that he would come back with help to remove his equipment. The backhoe, in fact, was stuck so far in the mud that no help he could muster would be able to budge this baby from its prominent spot smack in the center of our proposed lawn. If you are familiar with earth-moving equipment you know that they are painted one of the brightest yellows available. Well, this backhoe became our avant garde sculpture, its loud yellow body brightening up the drab muddy landscape. It stayed in place for six months.

During the period that the backhoe graced our yard, the swamp became even more troublesome. A huge tree, rooted on a steep slope on an adjoining neighbor's neighbors' property, had been leaning dangerously over the swamp ever since we purchased the place. It finally surrendered to the laws of gravity during a big storm, crashing down into the swamp. It was so large that it touched the other opposite boundary of our property. This event was on a scale that shocked even us, the pioneers who were at least in a decent battle with the main house. How could we handle this? Putting the cost aside, no tree removal experts would ever put themselves and/or their equipment at risk to tackle a job so fraught with danger and impossible removal logistics. Luckily, by this stage of our occupancy, we had discovered the magic of tool rental centers. These wonderful places had a complete selection of toys that untrained civilians would never own themselves. They actually let you take all kinds of stuff, from floor sanders to tractors back to your own place and do whatever pleased you. In this crisis we needed a big, big chainsaw, the kind you see out west in places like Oregon. Yes, we decided to take on the bad monster from the lagoon that had fallen into our beloved swamp. Armed with this big rental weapon, we waded into the swamp in old sneakers and old jeans, as we couldn't afford hip boots.

We sunk into the mud above our knees, and started the dismemberment. It went fairly well with the big saw ... what we forgot was the absurd business of removing all this heavy, wet wood from the swamp. We dealt with the branches, but the big fat logs were mired in the mud. Our only viable option was to purchase a pump, dig ditches and drain the swamp as best we could. This process required patience, not our strong suit. However, after about a month, the ground was firm enough for us to muscle the logs towards higher ground, both of us together. We should report that the property adjoining the swamp was a large estate which had a tennis court right in the other side of the property line. It also just happened that a spirited game of mixed doubles was being played at the exact time that we were wrestling in the mud with huge pieces of wood. When we heard comments like "good serve" or "great shot", we got laughing so hard at the contrasts in activities we could barely stop from falling down in the mud. Luckily, no errant tennis balls made their way over the fence into our swamp. It's a good bet that we would have been tempted to throw the mud-covered ball back onto the court, not a neighborly gesture.

The swamp continued to be a major source of consternation, intrigue and, occasionally, could be great fun. In the winter there was about a foot of water that meant we could ice skating virtually all winter. We took some home movies on an old brownie camera of the kid's ice skating on the swamp. One of the clips shows each child wearing one skate. We would run this movie at times with a narrative, saying that we were so poor our kids had to share a pair of skates. It goes without saying that our female Lab, "Georgie Girl" loved the swamp. All the fun aside, it was time to get serious and address the problem of a plugless body of water. We located an excavator who had the equipment and know-how to help us. He owned a large backhoe and explained that he would put down a "platform" of large timbers so his heavy equipment would be stabilized and able to dig a proper pond. This guy was heaven-sent. He worked quickly and created a huge hole exactly where we had envisioned the pond belonged. Even with such a wonderful accomplishment we had learned there may be a glitch. In this case, our excavator advised us that his other piece of equipment, a bulldozer, which he planned to use to spread the scooped-out dirt, had broken down and would not be available. The golden rule of fixer-uppers was invoked... "it's always something" ... a certainty that people our line of endeavor live with every day. This surprise left us with a twenty-foot-high pile of mud right in our front yard. It was the kind of soil you would expect from a swampy area, heavy and full of clay. Finding another operator to help with this problem was impossible, so we began to tackle the pile by ourselves.

The first experiment was shoveling the dirt into a wheel barrel at the top of this small mountain and wheeling it down a plywood roadway for dispersal around the surrounding land. To help with this system we hired a couple of strong teenagers. They lasted one half of one day, muttering things like, "Who are these crazy people anyway?" This reality check led us back to the rental toy shop where we hired a mini bobcat. We played with this adult toy for about a week (even letting the kids take a few turns) and managed to create some semblance of a level playing field. Then, once again, we returned to rental store where they entrusted us with a tractor that had what looked like a giant comb attached in the rear. This device was a "York rake" designed to take a rough dirt surface and beat it into submission. This phase of the operation was a big success, and we had a nice, level surface for a future lawn. However, the big hole for the future pond was still a gamble. As any reputable excavator will tell you, they just dig holes, they don't guarantee that they will fill up with water. Anxious owners must sweat this out. We lucked out. The hole filled quickly, and to celebrate, we made a trip to a pet store to buy a bunch of goldfish for their new home. The pond became a very special accomplishment for us, especially because the starting point was a swamp that should have been a deal breaker. If we were able to beat the big bad swamp, maybe the whole undertaking had a chance.

Meanwhile, the house was in a state of stop/start/stop/start. Over the course of twelve years, there were so many weird and wonderful moments that it is virtually impossible to cram them all onto this story. One of our biggest concerns with the project was the fact that we had placed our kids in an environment that might scar them for the rest of their lives. After all, we lived in a total wreck and their peers were children living in comfortable homes in an affluent community. What about bringing kids to our home after school? Would it be embarrassing? On the one hand, it was good for our kids to see us work hard and to have them do chores, but our circumstances were so completely bizarre compared to the surrounding world that we worried whether our decision to buy the place was a healthy one for them. They are now fully grown adults with their own families, and we are sure they would love to tell you about their impressions. They have assured us many times that they escaped unscathed from the experience, and we believe them. We do know that the house was a big gathering place in their teen years, and a great spot for parties because there was no way to damage either the structure or contents. As a matter of fact, our home was praised one year in their high school yearbook, saying that our barn would be sorely missed.

So, if we felt fairly secure about the children, the adults (two of us) and the pets (three of them) were having a great time. Oh, we managed to add a dog and a cat to the head count early in the renovation. The dog was picked up by us at the local pound. She was a German Shorthaired Pointer, about six months old and blind in one eye. We named her "Samantha", but we called her "Sam" for the rest of her life. She was a great companion for our Lab. The two of them frequent waders in the swamp and then swimmers in the pond. As the. future lawn was still a carpet of dirt, the two dogs were always muddy, but as we lived in a barn, there was minimal concern. They spent most of their time indoors housed in the old stable area which now had a plywood floor. When they shed their mud, they were permitted in the house, with each dog allowed to share a bed with a kid. Perfect. Our new cat was a kitten, being an unsolicited gift from one of our babysitters. She apparently had seen this little thing in a disreputable home and decided that it deserved a better place to live, such as a barn. She was a pretty cat, which apparently worked to her disadvantage, as she became pregnant at one of the earliest ages ever recorded in the feline world. She decided to give birth in our only bathroom, choosing a snug location under the old claw-footed tub. This was a poor decision. We still had to use this tub. We shored up the tub's footing to ease our minds and the family of six new kittens fared very well. However, they did seem to have somewhat shorter legs and walked with kind of a waddle.

The barn undertaking became an object of curiosity, concern, ridicule, and sympathy among both our immediate family and distant relatives. By distant, we mean those living in faraway places. We discouraged visitations, because to see our operation would just reinforce their initial impressions of our insanity. Unfortunately, we were called upon to host a Thanksgiving gathering during our very first November. The place was in a state of chaos, with heavy demolition underway. Bags filled with plaster rubble covered the stable floor. Once we learned of our assignment, we did purchase an electric stove for cooking, but that was it. There were only a few chairs and tables scattered around the two first floor rooms. With each arrival the adult relatives were handed a stiff drink to cushion their shock. One of our aunts was especially impressed with our progress. She entered the living room and commented on the beautiful wallpaper we had selected. This decorative touch was, in fact, bright pink insulation stuffed between the exposed studs of the open walls. She walked up to one of the walls and touched the insulation. Her subsequent observations were kept to herself. Of course, as we discovered with our earlier visitors, everyone was cautiously polite, hoping not to offend their hosts. It took great restraint, which probably was unleashed once they were back in their cars. We imagined that the most frequent remarks must have been something like, "Can you believe that place?" or, "How can they raise kids in such a wreck?"

Another batch of relatives arrived the following spring to bear witness to our plight, no doubt inspired by stories from the Thanksgiving group. During this time frame, our roof was having a rough time. It had lasted through the winter since the freezing surfaces had effectively masked its many weaknesses. With the arrival of spring, the roof relinquished it waterproof status, becoming a source of new leaks each day. As we learned, water takes curious paths from its sources, so climbing around on the roof trying to patch suspected holes proved to be totally frustrating. Until we could afford a proper roof, we had to live in a porous world. When the relatives arrived, they were greeted with floors that were littered with buckets trying to catch all the drips. These drips tended to change direction, so you had to be nimble changing buckets. When we gathered in the living room, there were over half a dozen buckets, including one sitting on a coffee table. The drips provided an interesting musical background, each having its own note. Once again, our guests were trying to be polite, offering generalities about the place's potential. The bottom line to all this hosting was a reinforced pledge to work harder to show all these people that we were going to prevail. No run-down wreck was going to beat us.

We won. The barn became a house in its 12th year. Just as this landmark was attained, we had to move back into New York City owing to our respective jobs, at least temporarily. Like us, the house was not in perfect shape, but it was certainly rentable and for the next twelve years served as a home for several different tenants, all of whom thoroughly enjoyed the house's setting, pond, and privacy. It was our first experience as landlords, an occupation that suited our personalities and experience in service-related occupations. Their positive reactions gave us a great deal of gratification because they were objective. We regained possession of the house in its 24th year and, due to our uncertain career paths, we decided to put the house on the market. We entrusted the sale to a new broker, as Blanche had retired. She had stayed in touch with us for awhile after our collaboration long ago and later admitted she had trouble sleeping after we moved in, worrying about how we could possibly survive in the wreck, especially with two young children. We sold the house to a couple whose main interest was the great privacy and setting of the property. We had mixed emotions which were natural our total involvement with the barn. Rather than pine for our first love, we decided to treat our effort as both a major accomplishment and learning experience.

So, why did we write this story? We owed it to the barn. This downtrodden building turned out to be a game changer in our lives. Not because of the challenge it represented, but for a much deeper discovery of a new dimension within ourselves. It went way beyond our initial goal of survival and became the basis for our future conduct. When financial consideration necessitates a rock bottom starting point, you gain a degree of confidence and determination that does not occur when you start your journey from a higher level. This may be an exaggeration, but a piece of real estate gave us a strong belief that we could conquer any worst-case scenario that may come our way. We've always admired people who possessed confidence if it was accompanied by humility. Well, the barn certainly taught us humility. The confidence and belief in ourselves were like graduation presents. It became our job to put these gifts to good use.

We hope we've done that.

Dog Guarding Muddy Driveway

Love at First Sight

Ready to Rent

Appliances Included

Tilework by Novice Owner

Bad Coal Furnace

Good Coal Stove

Squirrel Warfare

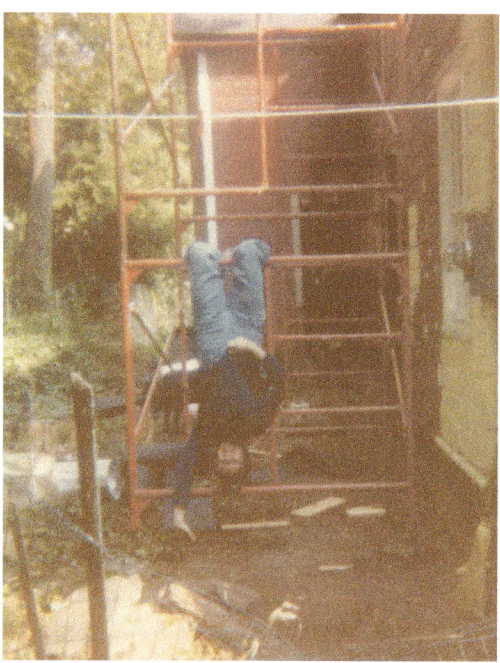

June takes a Lunch Break

Avant-garde Sculpture

Crazy Owner

Bad Swamp - No Plug

Good Pond

· A "Little Place" in the Country ·

If you have ever wondered about having a strange attraction to wacky behavior, don't worry. It happens to the best and worst of us. It is always a good thing to talk about uncommon endeavors. You will find more company than you expect.

In the 1980s our jobs required moving back to Manhattan. For the duration of this experiment, we decided to rent the barn, which somehow had become a very nice suburban residence. For our city habitat, we elected to purchase a co-op apartment rather than a rental. It was a relatively cheap and distressed unit within a building that was in the process of converting from rent controlled apartments to cooperative ownership. The barn had taught us that we could happily take on improvements that traditional city dwellers would never even consider. This next phase of our lives turned out to be almost as formative as our years in the barn conversion. Our lives were becoming more crowded and challenging. However, we did complete a few renovations, such as a new kitchen, making this small unit livable. One of us was a lawyer, and the other one decided to open a restaurant. Something he had never done and did not know the first thing about. With all this going on, we decided to sell the suburban home which had managed to survive its ordeal as a rental property in fairly good shape.

Why, then, were we so antsy? This phenomenon apparently is common with city dwellers, all of whom yearn for fresh air and a slower pace. Thoughts kept creeping into our minds, such as renting or buying a "little place" to escape to on weekends. In our case, we ruled out thinking about escaping to any seashore destinations … too expensive, too trendy, too everything. However, we had first met years ago at a summer spot in the Catskill mountains. This event was seared in our memories as both predestined and romantic. It was, therefore, completely understandable that when any thoughts about escaping from city life cropped up, it was only logical that visions of mountains appeared. We not only were infected with the desire to escape but had a built-in attachment to a particular destination.

In 1997, we took the plunge. Our initial idea was to look for an abandoned "farmhouse". We had selected an area in the northwestern Catskills that we knew to be non-trendy and affordable. Our intention was to have a typical little place in the country. Our miniscule budget meant that most prospective properties would be less than desirable. We contacted a local real estate agent whose specialty was dealing with city slickers and was known to have a stockpile of never-to-be-sold leftovers. We made a date to meet with her at her first selection which happened to be a farmhouse. Well, at the time, there were really no farmhouses as there were virtually no farms in the mountains. However, there were plenty of rundown dwellings sitting on untended rocky fields. Her first selection was not bad, but its location outside of any civilization was eerie. We were spooked. We realized that we needed some form of life and convenience. Suddenly, our dream blew up. Our veteran agent sensed this disappointment and quickly changed gears. She must have thought, why not show them one of the turkeys in the village?

She led us into the village and onto a road that quickly turned up a steep hill. There it was! Sitting on the top of the hill, like a beached whale. This thing blocked out the sky, an outrageous hulk sitting on a cramped lot. Our agent casually mentioned that it was 6,000 square feet and had 15 bedrooms. An unusual building that you would not want to escape to. Escape from would be more likely. We politely told her that we had run past our time for returning to the city and thanked her for her time.

She mentioned the asking price.

We decided to stay.

What the hell, we could do a quick walk through. We had never seen the interior of such a huge structure. It might be fun. Although the building itself had been built around 100 years ago, what we found inside was a museum dedicated to all the bad home decorating fashions in vogue during the 1950s. Nightmares throughout, such as glued down vinyl flooring and matching vinal wall paneling. Dropped-down ceilings with ugly asbestos panels. The only slightly different setup was the kitchen. Here, wallpaper was the main attraction. Because they had painted all the tables and chairs an alarmingly bright eye-catching yellow wallpaper with big brown flowers was added to pull the whole theme together. It had to be seen to be believed. Intrigued, we conducted a tour of the entire place, actually counting the fifteen (15) bedrooms which took some time, and the two (2) bathrooms, which took no time. Don't laugh. All we could think of were those long lines outside the commodes. At least, both baths were inside, not outdoors. The tour continued, each room decorated in a more courageous or outrageous manner than the last. It was also apparent that the prior owners had somehow obtained or inherited more furnishing that this structure could possibly hold. Wall-to-wall overstuffed chairs, requiring navigating everywhere through narrow paths. This tour could have lasted all day. Our salesperson-of-the-year realtor casually mentioned that all furnishings were included. How nice. The house was a bargain. The cost of removing all this stuff would cost a fortune. We politely thanked our agent for spending time with us and told her that we would give her a follow-up call in a few days. Insincerity at work.

We hopped into our getaway car.

Halfway home, we started to laugh. This was a sure sign that trouble lay ahead. We always lapsed into giggle fits before we did something stupid. Brains are not invited to these giggle sessions. We called and made a lower bid than the generously low asking price. Without even a pause, she indicated that our offer sounded fine and that the beached whale would be ours. A deal was made, the buyers giddy, the sellers even giddier. This was surprising because everyone involved in this transaction was taking a hit. The sellers were receiving less than anticipated, the buyers had just taken on a big building that had hundreds of secret construction flaws. It was really just a huge cavern waiting to have all that space expensively filled up. Oh, it also needed a new kitchen. Why was everyone so giddy? We don't have any answers ... it must be some nervous sense of humor that affects people who have just completed an exotic real estate deal. The sellers act like they have just escaped from prison. Buyers are awe struck, imaginations running wild dreaming about all the fun that awaits. The beached whale transaction was certainly bizarre. Everyone, including all the citizens in this small village, was dying to find out how these city slickers would tackle this brute. Us too.

There's not enough time or words to capture our thoughts at owning such a prize. Is it possible to be scared to death and excited at the same time? We had no idea how to start. We took the easy path ... pick one of the bedrooms to sleep in, clear out a space to cook in, and clean up one of the baths so we could clean up ourselves. How's that for a brilliant plan? All of this while hanging on to income producing jobs located over 120 miles away.

The best way to describe our awaiting challenges is to look at some of the photos attached. We have always believed that the kitchen should be the heart of the house. As you will see, it was a nightmare. It featured the wildest yellow colors ever seen in a place where human beings are supposed to enjoy peace and comfort. This important room became our top priority. Strip out the wallpaper, throw out the furniture, coal heating stove, ancient cooking stove, old refrigerator, and tons of unusable cookware and utensils. Repaint the wainscotting and floors. Rip out the dropped ceiling and paint the tin ceiling that was hiding underneath. That was our short list to provide not only a space to eat but also serve as our war room for tackling the roughly remaining 5,000 square feet of space that awaited.

We also started to think about this structure's history. Our realty professional believed that it originally served as a boarding house. This made sense, primarily because mountaintop cool weather provided relief from the city's unbearable, non-airconditioned heat. This explained the proliferation of boarding houses in the area. She had provided us with a postcard from either the original or early years picturing our new home approximately 80 years ago. This included a sales pitch stating, **"The Resort Beautiful ... for the vacationist who requires select, yet pleasing companionship and something different".** Well, how does this sound? Some of our neighbors' parents told them stories that the place was a house of "ill repute". Note that there were some attractive young ladies beckoning clients from the front porch. And, you could even make a reservation! We are mentioning this history to add some intrigue to a bland fix-me-up project.

The demolition/construction phase lasted enthusiastically for a few years. It just seemed longer. This place was the classic definition of "a work in progress". A job that you know will never be completed in your lifetime. Because we realized it would never be finished, perfection was never an option. We proceeded to invite large groups of families and friends, people with senses of humor who would appreciate staying in a never-to-be completed home. The only significant upgrade, other than the kitchen, was building a master bathroom. We borrowed two of the small bedrooms to create a large master bath with a huge shower/bathtub. While it was sad to reduce the bedroom count down to 13, we definitely needed a special place to clean up and feel somewhat human after working on dirty demolition jobs. Future guests would have to draw straws to gain admittance to this fancy room.

Again, pictures tell the story. What actually went on there will stay with the beached whale. Just know that it was exactly what we wanted. A daunting project, scorned by associates and local citizens. Anyone who knew about the nightmare of taking on big old houses must have thought that we were out of our minds. Well, they probably were correct, but our little secret was thinking that a little insanity was a good thing. Otherwise, every bit of work that went into these efforts would be for naught and these fine structures would slowly disintegrate, unloved and forgotten.

Beached Whale

Prior enterprise??

Painted to look smaller

1950's, nasty kitchen with ugly dropped ceilings

1990's, the brighter era of Laura Ashley. Tin ceilings exposed.

Vermont Castings Stove    Brighter Bedrooms

However, there were other risks that come with spending time in the mountains. You fall in love with the scenery. We would tour the countryside, often discovering never-seen-before landscapes and views. There was one special view that caught our attention. This was not good. We already had a nice, big place in the works. But this spectacular view also had a big, beautiful barn sitting right there, looking out for miles. Something clicked. It was a sinking feeling, like going to the senior prom with a perfectly fine date and having strangers catch your attention. Smart people recognize these distractions as superficial. Impulsive people see these as dreams come true. It was time to take a closer look at this beauty.

We know that you are shocked, truly shocked, that this mature couple would even think about taking on another Titanic. However, it was the view. Also, remember that we had already converted a barn into a house. We were therefore veterans and the recent purchase of the beached whale in the village had proven that size was not a problem. We did a rough measurement of the barn. It was over 100 ft. in length and about 40 ft. wide. With three floors, this would provide roughly 10,000 square feet of living space. Let's find out if it's for sale.

It wasn't. Well, not really. The owners were uninterested but curious enough to hear what these naive city folks might have in mind. Surprisingly, both parties were in the same ballpark and a deal was not out of the question. We had to demonstrate that we had enough credibility both financially and historically to take on a project of this size. They were rightfully determined to sell only to parties who would treat this special property with the respect and care that it deserved. Apparently, we passed the test. We became the proud parents of 10,000 additional square feet, bringing our current grand total in this village to 16,000 square feet. Oh, we did have something called occupations in the city downstate, but ho hum. Things were cooking in the mountains.

Woe is us. We now owned two "little places" to run away to. Are you still with us? Were we in over our heads? Probably. That's our definition of a comfy place. We obviously had to start working on the barn and the only logical solution was to use the beached whale as our headquarters. We would bear the cost of heating this smaller building for the duration, and then hopefully sell this partially improved property to cover some of the costs and cost overruns that will certainly be incurred at the barn. Economically, pretty scary. We never said that our decisions were either researched or wise. We just jumped in.

We believed that if cows lived there and were happy enough to produce quantities of fresh milk, this retirement-aged couple should be able to survive within these beautiful walls. Now, began the interesting job ...we had no idea how to begin. We grabbed a few pencils and began to draw lines. A kitchen here, a big great room with towering fireplace, a number of bedrooms scattered here and there, bathrooms galore, a big pantry room, a huge laundry room, on and on. Then we used the erasers on those same pencils. It was almost too much space. We gradually worked these drawings down to a reasonable configuration and one that would hopefully not collapse. We presented our drawings to a reputable architect who marveled at our creativity. He had never seen so many bathrooms and even a silent-butler to transfer laundry between floors! Reluctantly, he used our plans to secure the necessary building permits.

Where to start? What would you do? Call the realtor and sell? We decided to do what we do best. Clean. Starting with the cow parlor on the ground floor. Actually, dairy cows had great hygiene and their quarters had been routinely washed and cleaned. The fun started on the main floor where the farm machinery and miscellaneous objects had done serious damage. Also, wild critters and all types of birds and pigeons had resided there without interruptions. Way up high, there were numerous holes in the metal roof. We learned that this was typical with abandoned barns, as teenagers used their .22-gauge rifles to shoot pigeons in the rafters. Their missed or "through-and-through" shots found their way to the open skies. We also learned that these holes do not create big leaks, because the bullets would curl the tin roof outwards, versus a bullet that entered from the other direction. This is the kind of the good news discoveries that new owners, especially novices, love to hear. The entire main floor that had housed all the machinery was especially forbidding. It consisted of two layers of thick hemlock planks. The top layer had sustained heavy damage from wear and tear, so it had to be removed by hand, piece by piece and carted away. That little job was all ours. Thankfully, this was the only major demolition task, as the interior space was wide open. Normally, there would be all sorts of walls and obstructions to be removed. We were starting with big open spaces, leaving all the beautiful posts and beams in place. A nice first inning, but this game would be going into extra innings.

Wait a second. Who's going to build this place? Surely, we had some experience with demo and restoration jobs, but this was way out of our league. We decided to avoid big construction outfits, as they always seem to be thinking about the next project while leaving the work to lieutenants who may or may not be there to finish our job. Fortunately, we had used a great local carpenter for some work on our beached whale in the village. We talked with him about this job, and, surprisingly, he had always wanted to tackle a barn conversion and was delighted to join us in this scary undertaking. His confidence was supported by having a strong team of helpers and experienced local contractors for heating, plumbing and electricity. His big assignment was understanding that our goal was to create comfortable living quarters that would not compromise the spaciousness of the barn. We would be responsible for kitchen and bathroom designs and fixtures. As in each one of our prior rehabs, where we never used "designers", we would be selecting all of the critical materials such as flooring, windows, and tiles. For the gigantic fireplace, we already had chosen the mason and would be working with him to select the appropriate New York State granite for this important job. Plenty of toys for all of us.

We decided to work from the outside in rather than inside out. The entire building had to be waterproofed. This meant new boards and battens for nearly every side of the barn. A tedious job that involved renting a hydraulic lift. This wonderful machine was employed on so many of our future projects with windows and roofing, the neighbors must have thought we owned this big machine. You don't want to know the total number of windows that this job entailed. We won't tell you anyway. It's too embarrassing. We were determined to do the work properly because more than half of these windows would be providing killer views, especially at sunsets. Once this project was underway there was a built-in tendency to deal with current needs. It was never a good idea to look too far into the future. Baby steps were just fine. Colossal jobs like putting a new roof on top of this creation were never discussed.

First things first. We needed a pickup truck, one that could handle the rough terrain and heavy loads. We like to buy used trucks because of the cost and the simple fact that they take a beating with demolition loads. We picked a six-year-old Dodge Ram 1500, a bruiser. Funny, but this wonderful, tough vehicle put us in a combative mode ... we could never show up at this job site with some wimpy auto worrying about dings and dents. Plus, something called winter was coming and we were in a mountain range that routinely sets new snowfall records. Rugged four-wheel drive trucks become lifesavers. You don't go into battle with peashooters.

Amateurs tend to start projects of this magnitude at the wrong time of the year. Especially in the Northeast. Mid to late summer seems to be the most convenient time for these beginners. Quickly dropping temperatures would shut down vital installations such as heating and plumbing, insulation and curing of concrete. In other words, a stupid start to a job that required serious planning. Our wonderful carpenter and mason, both of whom already harbored concerns about our ability to pay for this massive undertaking, shrugged off our poor timing as their penance for even taking on this job in the first place. They would deal with a partially enclosed construction project with the same degree of patience that always comes with working with amateurs. They would shift their attention to smaller indoor projects with other customers, leaving us to complete the big job of ordering all the material and supplies that would be delivered later as permitted by the weather.

At this juncture of our story, we realized that it would be onerous for both of us to go into great details about all the unusual challenges that rookies face when taking on such a mammoth project. Just know that there were enough cliffhangers and setbacks that would deserve a separate, more voluminous telling. Therefore, we'll let the photos do the work. However, to give you a taste of these adventures we want to share a few of the events involved in the installation of the massive fireplace located in the "great room" with its 26-foot-high ceilings. If you are wondering about how this fascination with "great rooms" existed before this purchase, please refer to any architectural magazine that features these beauties. You never purchase these magazines, you just peruse them, either in a bookstore or in an orthopedic surgeon's waiting room. In either case you want to live in a place where this special feature is available. You picture yourself sprawled on a big comfy sofa with your dogs around you, taking in the warmth of a huge fireplace that has a beautiful stone chimney reaching into the sky. That was us. All we had to do was make the dream come true.

Because the fireplace was so important, we relied upon the knowledge and experience of our selected mason. We agreed that the most appropriate stone would be New York granite. Once decided, it was our job to go to the supplier's facility in Albany to select the actual stones. We had no clue about size, weight, and colorization. We just knew it looked great in pictures. The sales staff was delighted to see us. Apparently, there weren't too many people in this part of the world that were about to build an indoor jack and the beanstalk. When you first set your eyes on something like large granite stones, there are competing sensations of fear and awe. How were we possibly going to be select the right stones, sizes and quantity? Luckily, people who do this for a living were not only knowledgeable, but able to take drawings furnished by our mason and accurately fulfill our order. Whew. The only remaining job would be transporting this unbelievable load to the site and selecting a delivery timeframe. It was wintertime, so it was agreed that if we had a mild winter, we would both take our chances on a delivery date prior to spring. Having the material onsite would, at least, allow us to start building the massive foundation on the ground floor that would carry the weight of the entire chimney.

A seemingly reasonable plan, but foolhardy. Weather changes. A large truck arrived and dumped a huge load of large stones and concrete blocks right at the main entrance to the barn, which happened to be on the second floor. The concrete blocks, along with a portion of the stones, had to be carried down to the ground floor where the foundation for the fireplace would be constructed. There were no stairs. Therefore, long trips around the barn with these very heavy objects was required by you know who. A job we readily accepted. Unfortunately, the winter, which had paused, decided to return with a rapid, bone chilling drop in temperature. The beautiful New York granite froze in place in a big pile, where it would sit patiently for another month or so. This little piece of mismanaging something as basic as the weather told us that we would have to had to be less impulsive and more prudent the rest of the way. This was going to be difficult.

As with every construction job, there were unforeseen delays. Our mason, who had already started building the footings on the ground floor, received an emergency call that required his attention. Unbeknown to us, he was young man whose artistry and reputation had reached well beyond our little mountaintop. His urgent request was from Carmel, California. It seems that a good friend of Mr. Clint Eastwood (who just happened to be Mayor of Carmel at the time) had learned about our mason and determined he would be the only person in the country qualified for this job. Apparently, a retaining wall on Mr. Eastwood's property had been damaged. The job required an artistic touch. Our mason gladly agreed, flew out and did whatever it takes to please a man who liked others to "make my day". The contrast of glamorous Carmel with our barn in nowheresville still makes us chuckle. Our guy did return and completed building a magnificent chimney and fireplace.

Actually, living in the barn was a once-in-a-lifetime event. Just know that we were never happier. The joy was self-induced because of the setting, which was beyond description. The spread of happiness to family and friends was as an unexpected and joyful bonus. Grandchildren loved the place, running around footloose, either inside the cavernous space or outside in 100 acres. They even roller-bladed in the tiled hallways and took turns riding in the silent-butler. They especially loved playing hide-and-seek games, but they usually had to be curtailed because some kids would never be found. It was like a visit to Playland. We measured their love for the barn by the degree of crying that took place when it was time to leave for their trips back home. When we started this adventure, we had no idea that so many human beings would derive so much pleasure and record so many wonderful memories.

By this time, we had concluded our jobs in the city and had moved full-time into the barn. We became involved in the community. The lawyer purchased an existing law practice and became a true country lawyer. The restaurant guy opened a small local establishment. Things were looking good. In our enthusiasm, we managed to overlook just one small detail ... we were in our 70's. The barn was a joy, but awfully big. Our occupations required time and energy. We were overextended. We knew that the only honest answer was to scale down to a less demanding lifestyle. Downscaling was something we had never tried. The toughest part of this revelation was thinking about selling the barn. We shared our thoughts with our family. Not surprisingly, the biggest objection came from the grandchildren, all of whom cried out "Don't sell !!!" Leaving the barn would be like leaving a big piece of us behind.

Well, it was time to move on. No, this not the end of our little story. It's just that we decided that it was not really a great idea to have two septuagenarians living active and demanding lifestyles in such a rural environment. Health or related problems required access to convenient facilities. Prudent behavior was never our strong suit. However, it was time to pass the barn on to buyers who would reap the full benefits of this very special property.

First sightings of the view and the barn

Closer look at this huge thing

Before

*Historic Beams
as Pigeon Landings*

After

Dream Comes True

June, Fred, and Larry sitting in the fireplace in the barn's great room

Daytime and sunset views

Are you still with us? What should our next move look like? We decided that a region nearer Albany would provide the degree of civilization and niceties that one normally requires at this tender age. We decided to look for a house in the greater Albany area. Nice geographics, on the Hudson, trains into New York City, lots of doctors and hospitals, etc., etc. All factors that normal people use to determine "best case" options. Therefore, we had a grown-up plan, but the challenge would be to act like grown-ups. Here, our true personalities interrupted this interval of rational thinking. It started innocently enough, when one of us said … "wouldn't it be nice if we could find a place on the water?" Meaning a lake or a river. This little utterance kicked off our search in the wrong direction. We could never afford waterfront properties because they are notoriously overpriced. However, we thankfully were now conducting this search in the era of the internet. We could scan all kinds of so-called waterfront locations and might even find a few that included manageable water, such as a pond.

Well, one such place did appear. The residence was unusual in that it was built in 1800. Over 200 years ago. George Washington was president! This was worth a look. We located the realtor and hastily arranged a visit. We drove down the driveway and a decision was made when we saw this beautiful stone house sitting there on a beautiful pond overlooking nearby mountains. A no-brainer. Polite, but short negotiations resulted in an agreement. Only one little problem delayed a closing. It seems that the current owner had permitted at least nine feral cats to live in the basement. Their smell remained. It had to be removed, or else, no deal. This problem was unexpected, but upon resolution we proceeded with a closing. Certainly, egregious problems awaited. Anything this old will have secrets. Annoying jobs, like a new roof, new furnace and a completely new kitchen could be reasonably forecast. Stone houses, especially ones that are this old, reek of charm, but are famous for their smaller rooms, lower ceilings, and ongoing need for upgrades.

A perfect place for a couple that had tackled similar challenges on much bigger places. Same problems, just smaller in scope. We could manage this. The tradeoff for an old stone house is luxury versus history and we felt that history was much more significant and meaningful, especially at this stage of our lives. Besides, money could not buy a setting like this, a beautiful big pond just a few steps from the house with gorgeous views, including sunsets over the nearby mountains. A fitting atmosphere to reflect upon life. At least, we were in an allegedly civilized part of the world.

We cannot possibly talk about this special place unless we tell you about some of our very first experiences that came with living on a pond. We had no idea what to expect. Like most beautiful things, we realized that the pond would need attention. The obvious maintenance problems would be weeding and dealing with potential flooding. However, the real action turned out to be battles over occupancy. Us versus geese and beavers. The flying critters were really the most tenacious. Like some wealthy human beings, they were interested in only being around in the summer months, flying south as soon as the thermometer told them to seek warmer climates. Therefore, they would always be here at the same time of the year when we wanted to enjoy the great outdoors. Geese think they own the joint. They are nasty and act like we human beings had no right to be here. Normally, we would be glad to share paradise, but it was their omnipresence that dampened the mood. They arrived uninvited and immediately engaged in fowl husbandry, nature's way of keeping the national geese population on the rise. Up to nine or so little goslings would soon appear. Their presence wouldn't have been so bad if it weren't for their insistence that our property was one big bathroom. They taught their little offspring that our nicely mowed lawns were their rightful commodes. Their careless droppings were treacherous. However, when the little goslings first appeared, it was amusing to watch their playful nature and their first attempts at flight. Our female Labrador was especially intrigued with having her very own flock of geese. Her many attempts to establish relationships were consistently met with rejection. Geese and dogs never make great buddies.

The other cohabitants of the pond were a different story. Beavers. Again, a species that sounds harmless. Never heard of a beaver that was threatening to a human being. As a matter of fact, they have been glamorized as cute little creatures who sing Christmas carols over the holidays. Well, that reputation fades away when you share a pond. The basic problem with beavers is the simple fact that ponds have outlets where water levels are controlled. Beavers instinctively dam up these outlets. This task is in their genes … they simply cannot resist the need to build dams. Therefore, you are cohabitating with creatures whose out-of-control instincts directly threaten any pond. Water levels require control and ongoing management.

A nice young beaver couple arrived at the pond soon after we moved into our own house. They were obviously pleased with this location and proceeded to build their large beaver house, luxurious by beaver standards. Naturally, they then turned their attention to the pond outlet. With seemingly little effort they managed to quickly build a very effective dam which caused the pond level to rise. As rookie pond owners, we were frightened. The only option was to tear down their dam and permit the water to return to its proper level. Well, this seemingly straightforward proposition became an almost daily ritual. The elderly human being would wade into the stream in the morning and tear down the dam. That very night the young beaver couple would leave the comfort of their home, swim to the outlet and rebuild the dam.

A disturbingly regular pattern of breaking and rebuilding the damn dam persisted. Winter arrived. The battle continued. The human being not only had to break up the ice but was forced to purchase a big pair of rubber hip boots to deal with the freezing waters. Mr. and Mrs. Beaver paid no attention to the lower temperatures and actually seemed more enthusiastic in knowing that their human adversary was cold and miserable. However, they were surprised at this particular human-being's tenacity. Out of frustration, they decided to demonstrate their anger towards this stubborn person. They selected a very large pine tree that stood close to the banks of the pond and proceeded to saw it down with their teeth. Yes, their teeth. It was more than a foot in diameter and those large beaver teeth toppled this large pine tree directly into the pond. Their message was twofold… don't mess with us and the pond really belongs to us. Our ancestors lived here. This final act of disrespect caused us to rethink our relationship. The beaver family must go. We found a solution that entailed moving these stubborn little critters to a new location, possibly even a better neighborhood. We never really got angry with either the beavers or the geese…they were just doing what mother nature demanded. We accepted their presence as part of the deal for living in paradise.

And paradise it was. Our version of paradise, anyway. A place that was built with lofty intentions but suffered not only the ravages of time but the unrest that comes with numerous changes in ownership. This same feeling of paradise applied to our prior "little places". Each one was a learning experience. If life is really an ongoing education, we had been earning our diplomas in real world classrooms. The historic stone house was an appropriate place for our education to wind down.

Having emerged mostly unscathed thus far, maybe it was time to think about a more grown-up existence. Our deliberations were influenced by several untoward health-related incidents. These circumstances brought us back to reality. Logic entered the game. Funny thing about logic, it usually shows up when you are vulnerable and miraculously turns into a guardian angel.

We decided that a community that accommodates senior citizens who cherish their independence would be a prudent choice. We signed up. Our best decision ever.

Just like human beings, the two fixed-up "little places" and the old stone house were created to provide comfort.

That's why we were all created in the first place.

First sight of the stone house, with gravel up to the front door

The revival, with June's gardens and new roof and driveway

Before

After

Cramped breakfast nook

New breakfast area with large windows and wide exposure

The pond...

· The Mysterious, Misunderstood and Mismanaged Restaurant Business ·

"You're crazy!" Thirty years ago, these were the words expressed to me by my sainted Mother, who happened to be eighty years old at the time. I was at the tender age of fifty-five. I had just informed her that I was going to open a restaurant, a business that I knew absolutely nothing about. I was encouraged by her evaluation, because I have always considered being "crazy" as a good thing.

Whenever I heard anyone tell me that I was out of my mind, I would get excited. It meant that I was on the right track. I had always used contrarian thinking to navigate my way through life. Faced with any fork in the road, I would invariably select a direction other than the beaten path. This behavior resulted in a truly checkered career. If you placed my earnings over the years on a graphic chart, it would look like the zigzags on Casey Anthony's lie detector printout. More than once, I took jobs for zero pay or minimum wage just to get my foot in the door of a new business. It should be emphasized that this type of thinking requires a high tolerance for risk and, if married, it is essential to have a rock-solid relationship that can handle rough seas. Armed with these two attributes, I ventured into the quicksand of restaurant ownership.

Why did I even entertain such a fantasy at a time in life when retirement was within sight and good things like grandchildren were blossoming? We have to flash all the way back to my teenage years to gain an understanding of my motivation. It must have been strong, because it simmered inside for all those years. Back in the 1950s, my parents decided to move from the suburbs to New York City. I was in my late teens, which I thought was prime time. I had a driver's license, a girlfriend, was a hot shot basketball player (or so I believed), and was a member of a gang, such as they were in the suburbs. The good life. All of this great stuff suddenly vanished, and I found myself stranded in a cold, impersonal city with no friends and no prospects. Poor me. What to do? Well, one of the first things was to explore my new turf. Our apartment was located between Third and Lexington Avenues. The Third Avenue Elevated Train, affectionately known as "The

EL" was still operating and the neighborhood was on the verge of transition with tenements sharing space with new luxury buildings. A perfect mix. Scattered underneath the EL there were plenty of bar/restaurants. As the legal drinking age at that time was 18, it was only natural that a lonely young man would explore these establishments. It was a revelation. The common denominator was that each place resembled the popular TV series called "Cheers". While they all had different appearances, the atmosphere inside was similar ... you immediately got the feeling that people were enjoying themselves and that there was good chemistry between the staff and the customers. I had never been to England, but the phrase "local pub" was one that favorably described a typical English pub where neighbors gathered. I concluded that these establishments that were New York's answer to Boston's "Cheers" and the English variety. This was a positive finding. I finally had discovered replacements for the gang and the girlfriend in the suburbs. My "research" of many establishments taught me that it was possible to feel comfortable even in a big, impersonal city. I found myself gravitating toward one establishment. A place called "Donahues", on Lexington Avenue. I don't know when it originally opened, but it felt like it had been there forever and would keep going forever. The bartender treated each customer like they were family. They always served great food. Nothing fancy, but consistently good. This special place became my home away from home whenever I was on a break from college or in my subsequent working days. I'm sure that this positive experience was magnified by the fact that I was at loose ends because of the move into the city. However, the discovery that there were places that human beings could go to and feel so comfortable was a simple truth that would not fade away. It remained stored away in my brain as a good thing to emulate. Yes, that's right... my motivation more than thirty years later was to open a place like "Donahue's".

Fast forward to Age 55. I was winding down a spotty business career. Lots of ups and downs, but never in business for myself. Corporate life was as advertised ... they use you; you use them. The gratification was earning enough income for the family to survive. It was a welcome responsibility. Well, as the kids' college tuition became history, maybe it was time to finally do something that was more of a calling than a paycheck. Rather than agonizing over all the options, I went directly to my gut, which cried out "Open a Donahue's, dummy!" Contest over. Where to start? The priority was to make sure our marriage would survive. Again, my luck held. Being married to an outstanding woman who had always been supportive, the answer was yes, we could handle anything that came our way. We could survive on June's income for the duration of the gamble. The kids had graduated from college and were strong, independent individuals. These critical considerations satisfied; the next step was cutting the cord at work. My last job was with a giant corporation. It was the least gratifying, because as I climbed up the corporate ladder, I became more removed from customers. This was not good. I wrote a letter of resignation, stating that if God had intended me to attend so many meetings, He would have brought me here as a conference table. Cord cut. Time to move on.

Armed with no plan, no back-up plan and mini resources, my adventure began. I had no idea where to start. How hard could it be? My extensive experience as a patron of bars and restaurants told me that the business was like a three-legged stool, with food, service, and atmosphere the supporting legs. If they all are not of the same length or strengths, the stool crashes and the injured customer never comes back. Sounds easy. The food leg would be relegated to a chef. I knew absolutely nothing about food or running a kitchen and had no intention of learning this end of the business. It was too complex and demanding. Some start ... I would be handing over an entire phase of the business to someone I didn't know. I didn't even have the basic knowledge required to interview such a creature. However, this was not the time to dwell on scary negatives. I naively thought that I had the service and atmosphere legs of the stool under some control. After all, I had been in service-related businesses and had gained some practical experience in construction and design. These skills, while they appeared nice on paper, proved to need serious upgrading to tackle the complexities of building and running a bar/restaurant. If I had stepped back now and if I had the benefit of hindsight gained years later, I would have confirmed the observation of all of my relatives and friends that I was, indeed, out of my mind. Not to worry. It was time to get serious. To shore up my shaky credentials, I decided to attend a bartenders' school. The idea was to land a job somewhere to learn this side of the business.

As it turned out, this was the best school I ever attended. I called and gave them my name and credit card number. During this conversation, they made sure that the spelling of my name was correct and was exactly the way I wanted it to appear of my graduation diploma. In that one historic phone call, I had paid my tuition in full, enrolled and graduated. Education had never been this cool. The actual course lasted two weeks. We worked with bottles of colored water mixing "pretend" drinks. A lot of the concoctions were exotic, like "Sex on the Beach", "Harvey Wallbangers," etc. My fellow students were about the same age as my children, maybe even younger. They all aspired to work in "trendy" places where the action was intense, and the nights never ended. Although I was a mystery to them, they thought it was great that a guy my age could keep up with this energetic group throwing colored water into glasses creating make believe drinks. Apart from being awarded with a diploma that was printed at the same time as my enrollment, my favorite thing was final exams. I scored 100% on all the tests, something that I had never achieved in 16 years of education. Not even close. Now, as a Cum Laude graduate, I entered the job market.

A rude awakening. Age discrimination was alive and well. I liked to think so, anyway, faced with rejection after rejection. Surely it was my partially gray hair, not my vast experience or star student credentials. How could they not embrace a hot prospect like me, other than the age thing? Chin up, I walked into a nice place on the upper Eastside. I told the owner that I was willing to work for free ... no pay, not even a complimentary meal. I was hired on the spot. He was a gambling man, allowing me to work the cocktail shift, catering to locals and regulars who dropped by after work. My kind of customer. My shift was scheduled to end around 8p.m. turning the bar over to a younger, more experienced bartender. Besides, it would be getting closer to my bedtime. To my delight, I found that I was comfortable behind the bar. Within about two weeks, I gained a "following", something that good bartenders are supposed to do. The owner was also pleased but suggested that my popularity may have been slightly enhanced by the fact that I poured a generous drink. Also, my inability to make correct change all the time may have been a factor. After all, I was a refugee from a corporate world where we wore suits and didn't do stuff like make change. My position at this restaurant became awkward when I confided to the owner that I was planning to open my own place. We agreed to a mutual (no fault) separation, wishing each other good fortunes. He was a seasoned owner, and he had the good grace not to warn me about the quagmire ahead. Anyway, I'm sure that I would have shrugged off any caution.

Being impulsive, my next move was to start looking for space. I had decided that our location would be on the Upper West Side, as this particular region of New York was in a state of renaissance. This meant that there might be greater opportunities for finding unusual locations in older buildings that were candidates for renovation. Timing would also be a positive factor as rents were generally lower than those in fully developed areas of Manhattan. With this curbstone business analysis resolved, I spent a few weeks stalking the entire region. It was during this survey that I suddenly realized how ridiculous it was to look for a place to house a business that was still a figment of my imagination. This is a built-in flaw for people like me ... we get excited about a challenge, become convinced that we can conquer anything in the wilderness, and then proceed to charge into an unmarked trail with no map or compass. While being impulsive can be troublesome, I like to think of it as a spark plug that gets things ignited. If this tendency is suppressed, nothing would be ventured. So, there I was, standing in front of an empty space when reality came crashing into my daydream. I was in no position to even take the first step in this undertaking. I did not have an incorporated business or any other evidence that I was a legitimate enterprise. I was unable to make any commitments whatsoever to a landlord. This reality check triggered other disquieting thoughts ... was I in over my head? ... did I need a partner? ...were my resources adequate?

Fate arrived just in time with some answers. We had made friends with a couple who lived in our West Side cooperative building. The husband served with me on the board of directors, and he was in the construction business. One night, after a stressful board meeting, we went out for a few beers. I mentioned the direction that my life was taking, and he surprisingly admitted that opening a pub-type place was one of his lifelong dreams. A partnership was born. The best part was the fact that it was created in a local saloon, sometimes a good place for bonding. Besides the obvious benefit that this individual was in the construction business, I derived a needed comfort level that there was another human being out there who was just as crazy as me. I resumed my search for space with renewed energy.

I learned that the selection of space to fulfill your dream (investment) was strikingly the same as finding a place to live. A visceral reaction has to occur. With a house, it's something like the view, the layout, the kitchen, or whatever. You know immediately that this is it. Welcome to the similar world of retail commercial space. You must have a gut feeling that an empty space would be compatible with the atmosphere that you intend to create. A few days after the new partnership was formed, I was wandering up Columbus Avenue and spotted a vacant store that was actually slightly elevated above street level. It was a corner space and had a short flight of outside stairs directly from the sidewalk on Columbus. The building itself was a beautiful century old structure that apparently had fallen on hard times. There was graffiti along with other signs of either neglect or aging. It was perfect. This was it. I called my new partner, and he rushed to the space and agreed on the spot that this would work. I contacted the broker who was handling this building and he advised me that the landlord was adamant about not having a food establishment as a tenant. Undaunted, I pressed for a meeting with the landlord and, surprisingly, he agreed to meet with us. It was a wonderful meeting. For some reason, this veteran real estate owner took a liking to us. I think he was pleased that I had some gray hair and wore a suit. Style over substance. We convinced him that we would be making substantial improvements to the space and the exterior of the building. I learned a valuable lesson in negotiating with landlords. While it is important to establish your credibility, it is equally vital that you treat the relationship as a partnership, with a commitment to work closely to make the enterprise a success. If the tenant does well, the overall reputation and value of the building is enhanced. Who could argue with that? We agreed to a lease that contained reasonable terms and a generous build-out time frame.

Very good. We had managed to secure prime space in a great location. We had a top-notch construction company ready to build the place. Not bad for a couple of idealists new to the business. You would think that the next phase should be easy. Wrong. The nightmare called bureaucracy was in our path, an impenetrable mountain of paperwork and regulations typical of big city governments. They love to test your patience and staying power. Architects, lawyers and accountants feed on them. Our celebration at having snared a prime location suddenly became an unwanted storm of paperwork, adding cost and time to the project. Work permits, liquor license, health department permit, landmark building regulations, on and on. This second dose of reality prompted us to consider bringing in an additional partner. Strength in numbers and finances were required. Months ago, I had already spoken with a friend who had worked with me at the giant corporation about my future plans. He welcomed the idea of joining us as a consulting partner, while retaining his corporate status. He also was going to contact another friend who might be interested in working with us. It was encouraging to know that other people did not brand us as whackjobs and were willing to sit in the front seats of the roller coaster along with us.

Bolstered with additional resources, we began to tackle the 100-year-old building. The former tenant, a woman's clothing store, had trashed the place. They should have been sentenced to jail for having such bad taste. They painted over the beautiful brick walls and covered the large, unique arched windows. Sinful. The demolition phase was enjoyable, ripping out their bad stuff and revealing an outstanding, unusual space to work with. It was comprised of two large rooms, each with fourteen-foot ceilings. The room with the entrance door would make a perfect bar, with a wood burning fireplace and ample room for furniture and tables. The adjoining room with the large arched windows, was ideal as a dining room. As we looked at the bare bones space after gutting the place, we were struck by its size and architectural beauty. It was almost too nice for the comfortable local neighborhood place we envisioned. We probably could have stopped right there and sold our lease to a legitimate restaurateur who could then build a first-class operation worthy of the space. That was not an option.

What to build? The more we looked at the empty space, the more we struggled with a plan. One day we were standing around looking for inspiration, and I was struck by the thought that the whole space resembled a house, with the bar being the indoors and the room with the windows being an outdoor, or patio area. We decided to build a house inside of a building. This just proved that sometimes an initial idea often morphs into a different outcome. My intention to create a "local" pub type place was somewhat compromised by the new development of having a house inside the building, but the nature of the space made this the only logical option. So, we built a wall at one end of the proposed dining room to house the kitchen. This wall became the outside of an actual house with cedar siding, a shingled roof and a chimney. In the center of the wall was a nice big window, with shutters. This would be the opening from the kitchen to the dining room. Food would be passed through the window, for waiters to distribute to tables. No kidding. The concept was whacky, for sure. For customers to buy into the idea that they had entered a patio through French doors from the bar room, we painted the ceiling in the dining area a sky blue, with some clouds. No, the clouds did not move. The whole thing seemed to work, however, and the intention of creating a home away from home was satisfied. The bar room with its fireplace and comfortable furniture was definitely in sync with the cozy feeling we envisioned. It created an immediate feeling of comfort as you walked through the front door. We were unconventional rookies building a one-of-a-kind bar/restaurant in one of the most demanding and sophisticated cities on the planet. This had to be one of the most incredible tests of risk tolerance ever recorded.

Personnel. Why does this word send tremors through the ranks of business owners? Why does the seemingly pleasant task of dealing with other human beings become such a burden? Restaurants, in particular, have a scary reputation. I had heard the complete gamut of warnings, such as "the turnover will kill you" or "they'll steal you blind", etc. etc. None of the dire forecasts bothered me. We were about to open a place where people would want to work, and we would trust our employees rather than treat them as untrustworthy. If you treat people with respect, you vastly increase the odds of them respecting you. This was going to be my laboratory for testing these theories. As the story unfolds, you will learn how my idealistic experiment played out.

The first challenge was finding a chef. Through networking we contacted a lovely young lady, who enjoyed an excellent reputation in terms of her skills and temperament. Her background was a good match for the type of cuisine we had in mind. Luckily, she agreed to join us, as this was an opportunity to oversee a manageable operation, rather than working in the pressure cookers found in high-end New York establishments. We described our operation as a neighborhood place where we would be serving comfort food rather than pretentious fare. She was our first hire, as a good deal of pre-opening work had to be accomplished with setting up the kitchen and lining up staff. She proved to be a great team player, putting up with our lack of experience, yet excited about being part of such an unusual experiment. The recruitment of other staff was a different challenge. More people, more backgrounds, more personalities. Experienced wait staff and bartenders were skeptical regarding new restaurants. Rightly so. However, many of them had been working in places that were poorly managed or had overbearing owners. We may have been new, but we talked a good game and espoused a friendly atmosphere where teamwork would prevail. Somehow, we managed to enlist a solid core of professionals who would gamble along with us. They would wait for our construction to be completed before giving notice to their current employers. The personnel issues we had feared were proving to be less draconian than anticipated. They were sure to crop up later.

Enter the mysterious world of purchasing restaurant equipment and furnishings. It became immediately apparent that we could not afford to buy any new stuff. Enter the equally unknown world of auctions. I forgot to mention that we were about to invest our life savings in not only a crazy speculation, but at a time when the economy in the city was in the tank. This meant that a great number of restaurants were closing, with numerous auctions of restaurant contents taking place. Because of our budget we were going to resort to buying stuff we weren't sure would even work. It was similar to having a person who knew nothing about automobiles do the buying at a car auction in the Bronx. You are really not a restaurant veteran unless you've attended some of these auctions. The action is intense, and the competition is fierce. There's always a number of used-equipment dealers eying bargains and picking out the best stuff. Then, there are novices like me with a long list of goodies and little money. Purchasing all the tools of the trade for the dining room and bar were my responsibility. Left on my own at many auctions, I managed to gather a bazaar collection of merchandise. There were practically no matching sets ... dinnerware, silverware, glasses, tables, and chairs, all had their own personalities. I rationalized these purchases by convincing myself that it would create a stir among our customers. You know, when you are first seated at a restaurant, you look at things like the silverware and glasses and the fact that they bore no resemblance to one another gave them something to talk about. It was definitely a new wrinkle to the boring table setup. Besides, the classic goods were way beyond our means.

My one outstanding purchase was pure luck. I had always yearned for a copper-topped bar but realized that this luxury was a pipe dream. No way. Then, at what seemed to be just another routine auction, our luck changed. The place was Joe's Pier 52, a landmark seafood restaurant located on 52nd Street. When I walked in, there it was ... a copper-topped bar with a beautiful oak base, obviously built by master craftsmen. There was a slight problem in that it was over 80 feet long, divided into large sections. It was being auctioned as one entity. We only needed about 30 feet. I estimated that it must have cost around forty thousand dollars to build and install. I called my partner and told him that the bidding would probably be in the six-thousand-dollar range. We agreed that this was way beyond our reach. Out of curiosity, I stuck around until the bar was scheduled for auction. No one bid. In shock, the auctioneer reluctantly dropped the opening price to five hundred dollars. I raised my hand. We won at this ridiculous price. I called my partner, breaking the news and asking him how we could get this massive thing out of here? It was a logistical nightmare. No wonder no one bid. We contacted the construction crew that was working at our site, and they managed to arrange for a truck and somehow dismantled the bar. We had to store the sections that were more than our required thirty feet, and ultimately sold these extra pieces for more than our cost, including labor. This was my one and only major victory on the auction battlefield.

So, with the staff on board, and the place somewhat furnished, we were in a fairly good position to OPEN. A few minor problems remained. We had failed to decide upon a name of the place and had absolutely no marketing plans in place to announce this important event. I brought up the fact that the neighborhood had been watching us for months and they continually fawned over my partner's female golden retriever who had sat patiently on our front stairs for the entire construction period. We agreed to name the restaurant after this wonderful dog. A friend did a rush job on a logo design and two small, low-key signs were made up and placed outside. We agreed that our place was not going to be a trendy hot spot, so a splashy opening was not appropriate. Our marketing plan was simple ... open the door.

"Phoebe's" was born on a rainy Tuesday night.

For about an hour, no one came in. We envisioned our investment vanishing down the drain. At last, our first customers, a group of eight, came through the door. Apparently, they had just come from a funeral parlor, and their somber mood did not resemble an Irish wake. I could sense some concern among the staff that they had left their secure jobs to work on the Titanic. Then, a few more people trickled in, followed by a surge from the neighborhood. Apparently, word had gotten around that "Phoebe's" was open at long last. There must have been serious pent-up demand for a decent local pub-type place, because we became an overnight phenomenon, totally unexpected and unprepared. We were obviously pleased with the welcome, but honestly overwhelmed. Luckily, our seasoned staff handled the volume of activity in their stride, as did the kitchen. Remember the principle of the three-legged stool ... food, service, and atmosphere? Our greatest concern was gaining favorable first impressions on all three of these critical elements. It seems that we were either better by comparison than anything in the area or we really did satisfy our customers, because we received very positive feedback from day one. Whew!! We were determined not to let this initial blast of popularity go to our heads. The last thing we wanted to be was a trendy "in" place. By definition, trendy means short-lived. Our mission was to be a local, comfortable gathering place, a "safe harbor" from the rigors of city life. We reaffirmed our commitment to the neighborhood and settled in for the long haul.

The biggest adjustment for us rookies was the pace and unforgiving hours of running a restaurant as a business. The fun stuff of greeting customers and witnessing them having a good time kept our motors running and stoked our enthusiasm. However, the reality of keeping this wonderful new machine well-oiled and capable of such a sustained effort proved to be an unforeseen challenge. The best analogy I could use would be a swimmer at an ocean beach, where you have just been hit by a big wave and are in the process of trying to get the sand out of your bathing suit when another big wave comes along and smacks you down. It never stops. The first year of operating any new business is a mind-numbing experience. A restaurant has its own set of quirks and ongoing problems, exacerbated by the need to be open seven days a week. You never get a chance to catch your breath.

Earlier in the story, I had mentioned my idealistic experiment with the staff which entailed creating an atmosphere of trust and teamwork. This plan had mixed results. The two sensitive issues with the wait staff were how to handle tips and who would work the best shifts. Fun stuff. I imposed a pooling of tips to create the maximum environment for teamwork. I stumbled through the problem of shift assignment as best I could, given our newness, with no seniority criteria. Neither of these policies received unanimous support, but, somehow, we survived without any compromise in the quality of our service. Thankfully, business was brisk, and it *was* a nice place to work. These two factors meant that we were retaining quality people despite all the dire warnings about staff turnover.

The kitchen staff was a pleasant surprise. Here the key was respect. Working long hours in a hot kitchen, and especially a small one such as ours, is a tough job, both in terms of preparation and intense pressure during peak demand. While the prime motivators of any professional chef are to create great food and have their work appreciated by customers, it is equally important let them know how much they contributed to the success of the enterprise. The rest of the kitchen staff must also believe that their work was valued. Because of our small size, we all had to perform extra chores when there were staff shortages or when some crisis happened in the middle of a shift. For example, in the restaurant business it is a cardinal rule that equipment always breaks down at the most inopportune time, such as during peak business demand. On a number of occasions, I found myself washing dishes by hand alongside a worker when the automated dishwashing machine decided to breakdown. These built-in crisis situations gave our staff a new look at "management" in action, decidedly different than they had experienced elsewhere. I believe that they respected us. For sure, we respected them. If I had to grade our performance during that first year, I would have to give us a "C" Plus, earned mostly because of effort, not smarts. On an education track, we were about senior high school level, with admission to a top college not bloody likely.

I'd love to go on and on with stories about our experiences, mistakes, and lessons. We never took ourselves very seriously, so these episodes were too numerous to relate in this short story. However, I will share a few, just to give you an idea of how the place functioned. The first lesson we learned was that your customers generally reflect that type of place that you have created. For instance, a high-end restaurant attracts you know who. A dive draws dive aficionados. We were somewhere in the middle. We designed the place to be a neighborhood "local pub", and by and large, this was the outcome. Certainly, the bar area with its wood burning fireplace and cozy furniture was a big hit, especially in the winter months. We did have an unusual dilemma, though, soon after opening. A food critic from New York Magazine apparently had been checking us out and wrote a very flattering article about "Phoebe's". We were slammed with new business. Normally, this type of positive publicity is something most restaurants would kill for. Not us. Customers were coming from every far corner of the city and through tunnels and over bridges to get here. They even came from the more upscale East Side to check us out. Of course, there were the trendy types, anxious to find a new "in" spot. The net result of all this activity was an infusion of customers who probably would never return, either for reasons of convenience or the simple fact that our place was neither upscale nor trendy. We had an artificial jolt of business on our hands that sorely tested our staff and facilities. More important was the fact that our regular customers could not get into the place. This was very bad. We had always embraced the philosophy that if we delivered on our promise to be a quality driven local establishment, we could survive on local good will and positive word of mouth. We learned that favorable publicity did, in fact, compromise our mission. Strange but true.

For some reason, we had an unusual number of celebrities who liked "Phoebe's". Maybe they just got tired of being pestered by other customers when they went to other restaurants. Because of our low-key environment and the laid-back attitude of our customer base, they probably felt like we were a "safe harbor". Hooray! Remember our goal? Occasionally, they even got lost in the shuffle during one of our hectic shifts, Surprisingly, Sunday Brunch had become one of those popular shifts. There was always a long line outside with a serious waitlist. Lucky me, just about every Sunday, I got to handle the door and work the waitlist, facing hoards of hungry and impatient people. On more than one occasion, I failed to recognize famous stars of stage, screen, and TV. In hindsight, I justified my performance as being totally democratic in keeping with our policy of treating each customer equally. In reality, had I recognized them, I'm sure that I would have at least found a spot for them at the bar and would have handed them a Bloody Mary to make their wait more palatable. I also rationalized that jumping their name on the waitlist would have violated the trust of other customers, kind of like cheating on a ski lift line. No way. Besides, recognizing them in real life is hard. I had no paparazzi skills. I may have screwed up under severe brunch pressure but took solace in the fact that these nice people still loved our place. No, I am not telling you who I managed to miss.

Somehow, we survived the critical start up years of our fledgling enterprise. As we entered our adolescence, the reality of running a day-to-day operation created a new challenge and the need to create a plan for sustaining the business over the long term. Historically, restaurants have a rough financial time in the first few years. We were not the exception. To make sure that we were creating the best possible first impressions and earning customer loyalty, we employed a larger staff than necessary and did not adhere to industry budget guidelines for food and other purchases. I was the idealist, enthusiastic about our acceptance and willing to defer better business practices until we were further along the path. My partners were more businesslike and wanted to tighten our operation. This was not an impasse, merely a philosophical difference. However, it caused me to reflect upon my strengths and weaknesses and how they related to "Phoebe's". As the "senior" partner, my role was primarily dealing with creative matters and business deals such as lease negotiations. I was also the largest investor and came up with additional funds when we encountered cost overruns during the build-out. Because it was my impulsive nature that got us into this adventure in the first place, the degree of investment was certainly appropriate. What became apparent was the incompatibility of my personality with the day-to-day operation of a restaurant. I was not a maintenance person, nor was I interested in detail such as cost controls, vendor relationships, and all the minutia involved in a business that operates 364 days a year. After the first few years, it was time to take an honest look at my future. My original partner had already sold his interest and was back to concentrating on his construction business. I concluded that my dream of creating a "safe harbor" gathering place had been achieved. Three years after the opening of "Phoebe's" doors, I sold my interest to the remaining partners.

I'm sure you're thinking why did this guy work so hard and then jump overboard just when the ship was under full sail? Well, it went beyond my discomfort with the administrative responsibilities. My only rewarding times at "Phoebe's" were when the place was full of customers enjoying themselves. As we were only open for dinner, this entailed being there at night. The prospect of having no family life was unacceptable. I treasured my nights and weekends with my wife and family. Because of the disorientation that takes place when one is consumed with a project like this, I had completely blocked out this obvious conflict of interest. My decision to sell was the right thing to do.

The good news was the discovery that I thoroughly enjoyed being the principal instigator and founder of a new business. I also learned that my major strengths were with creative challenges and overcoming start-up problems. In addition, I realized that someone my age and experience was able to help create new enterprises hand-in-hand with young professional people who had the skills but lacked the resources to open their own businesses. The concept would be to use my start-up experience to establish a place and then have the young professionals run the operations with an agreement to eventually take full ownership.

This seemingly simple conclusion led to a blueprint that would enable me to open three additional local "gathering place" restaurants over the next 15 years.

After the roller coast ride, my adrenalin supply was diminished, but I still needed activity to keep my "late middle aged" constitution in playing condition. We had always been fond of the northwestern Catskill Mountains. We met there in 1960, and always planned to have a second home that might become a permanent home after having lived there on a trial basis. Our plan was to look for a piece of land with a farmhouse that needed work. We ended up buying something entirely different ... a house located in a small village. It wasn't a house in the traditional sense. Back in the heyday of the Catskills, it served as a boarding house. It was over 6,000 square feet and had 15 bedrooms. It was in terrible shape and in need of serious updating. Perfect. It was not only within our budget, but the extensive rehab work would keep me out of trouble for at least a couple of years. A wonderful distraction following 30 years in the business world and three years in a whirlwind known as the restaurant business.

Flash ahead to age 61. I got the itch to open another place. I had easily identified the quirk that drew me to this next adventure. Whenever we went to a restaurant, I would look around and be astounded at the mediocrity that prevailed, regardless of the rating or reputation of the establishment. My criteria for having all three legs of the stool (food, service and atmosphere) of equal quality was never met. There were always shortcomings. I found it hard to suppress my astonishment that these places were lacking in one or more of the criteria, and in doing so, the experience of every customer was being short changed. I became excited about correcting this commonplace mediocrity and opening another place was the only logical way to do so.

I've got to take a break here and express some of the feelings that I am experiencing as I tell this story. I have just concluded that it would be wearisome for both of us to have me go on and on in detail about the last three restaurants. They all seem to follow a pattern, anyway, as far as finding the space, struggling through the build-out, and, finally, the almost anti-climactic business of running a restaurant. As I thought about my second place, I realized that this is the one that touched me profoundly. It was the only one that embodied all of the character and qualities that I had envisioned when this journey began. This realization was a clear message that I should spend most of the time talking about a place that was special from the very start and which remains today as an endearing legacy. Of course, I will go on to say a few words about the last two restaurants. They actually were opened, much to my surprise because I was exceeding the allowable mileage for this kind of exhausting endeavor.

Here is the story about "Fred's".

Where to locate? We had become comfortable living on the Upper West Side, and it made sense to look in an area that was compatible with our lifestyle. "Phoebe's" was finishing its seventh year of operation and was in the process of transforming itself into a nightclub, including expansion. There was no conflict with a new place that would be a respectful distance away and based upon a different concept. In my neighborhood walks, I had noticed a place that had an enclosed entrance which contained stairs down to a level several feet below the sidewalk. It was obviously closed and had a sign taped to the inside of the enclosure which claimed that the place would be opening again after renovations were completed. There were no indications that any work had been started and that notice had been there for several months. There was a big, big sign attached to the building over the entrance which loudly proclaimed the place to be "Singapore Sally's". Sally herself was portrayed in a tight-fitting dress and a come-hither posture. A classy place. It was perfect. I decided to contact the landlord to ascertain whether the space might be available. The landlord advised me that the lease was still active, but the tenant may be interested in subletting or selling the business. I immediately contacted the tenant, who reluctantly agreed to a meeting. He admitted that he was having a hard time obtaining the landlord's approval for candidates he had presented to take over his lease. I decided that this was a very special opportunity for space in a desirable neighborhood. I outlined a deal with the tenant. We agreed in principle, and he arranged for a meeting with the landlord to present me, his new candidate. It turned out that, like most landlords, this one was also interested in any tenant other than a food establishment. Despite my suit and mature appearance, I did not receive a warm welcome. The landlord was a well-established company that had vast holdings on the West Side. The principle was a seasoned professional, a gentleman who took pride in his dealings. Also in attendance was his nephew, a nice young man, recently married. After the usual introductory sparring and admonition about restaurants in general, they got around to asking me about my background. I started off by stating that I was the founder of a place on Columbus Avenue called "Phoebe's". The nephew almost jumped out of his chair and said, "That's our very favorite place ... we go there all the time!" In my entire life I had never achieved an advantage so quickly. This was one great way to start a negotiation. The landlord gave a verbal approval, subject to the usual background checks. Also, the current tenant sweetened our separate deal because he had finally found someone to take over the space that was acceptable to the landlord. These incredible positive developments told me that the next adventure was meant to be.

Once again, my ingrained impulsive nature had led to a stage in the process that was well ahead of any concrete, well thought out business plan. I had a place to do business but did not have any of the other requisites to go forward. The primary missing ingredient was one or more young, experienced professionals to sign up as partners. I had several candidates, but my top prospect was a young man who had worked at "Phoebe's". I made sure that this was OK with my prior partner, and then entered serious discussions with this young man concerning the new place. He was enthusiastic, except for the fact that the space was in a "basement". He had shared his concerns with his fiancée and the three of us met to take a hard look at the space. The term "basement" was not really accurate. It was only a few steps below sidewalk level and there were large windows that people walking by would be drawn into by the lighting inside in the evenings. They would look in and see customers enjoying a candlelit atmosphere, conveying a cozy message. We all agreed that the space would work. A new partnership was formed.

I started to get really good vibes about this place. Surely, "Phoebe's" was an unexpected success and certainly was a learning experience. However, I never quite felt that it became the intimate "safe harbor" that I had envisioned. This may have been largely due to the space itself, with its large rooms and high ceilings. Now, we had something to work with ... the few feet below sidewalk level created an immediate sense of escape and mystery, like you were entering a special place reserved just for you. Before this transition could become reality, we had to deal with the business of removing sexy Singapore Sally from the premises. Her big sign outside was first to go. She was also painted on the wall inside and was accompanied by all kinds of ugly furniture and fixtures that came with our deal with the former tenant. Once again, it was a pleasure to gut the place and give the space a chance to breathe. All the walls had been sheet-rocked, covering beautiful 100-year-old brickwork, including a fireplace.

Before going any further, I want to tell you that I had already decided to call the place "Fred's". This was an easy decision. Fred was our one-year-old female black Labrador Retriever. She had a lot of good things going for her. She was bred by one of the most wonderful charities on this planet … Guiding Eyes For The Blind, located in Yorktown NY, a dedicated group of people who breed and train dogs as guides and companions for the visually handicapped. Because their standards are rigorous, some of the puppies and young dogs do not have the aptitude for this demanding role and are put up for adoption. Fred was one these adorable puppies and we became the lucky new "parents" after being in line for more than a year on a wait list. Guiding Eyes had already given her the tentative name of "Singer" largely based on her ability to wail louder than any of the other puppies in her litter. We had already decided that the name was going to be "Fred" regardless of the sex of the puppy that we may be fortunate enough to adopt. The name suited her well, and she was an immediate big hit in her new home in the city. If you've ever witnessed anyone with a small puppy on a leash walk the sidewalks of New York, you observed owners who could not get to their destination. Virtually every passerby stops to pet the cuddly little thing and the adorable pet responds with big time wagging of the tail and generous kisses. A nonstop show every few feet. She was a star in the neighborhood and a regular at the local dog runs. It was only logical, when the unconventional owner decided to open a restaurant/bar in the immediate area, that the place should be named after one of its favorite local residents.

Her name turned out to be a big deal. I originally thought that it was appropriate because of Fred's special breeding. There was a wonderful story to tell while simultaneously making the public aware of Guiding Eyes and the great work that they do. Also, the name was short, easy to remember and kind of rolled off the tongue when the common phrase "let's go to (blank)" is used. What evolved were additional meanings and dynamics surrounding the name. First was the reaction of dog owners, initially from the neighborhood, but ultimately from around the nation and overseas. These owners began to bring in pictures of their own dogs, framed and ready to be hung on our walls. They all were "autographed" and most had messages to Fred. One of my favorites was from a big Standard Poodle, saying, "Remember our night together in Paris?" This phenomenon continues to the present time, to the point where the premises have virtually run out of wall space. There are more than 1,200 framed pictures of Fred's friends hanging out at her place. It's quite a sight.

One big surprise involved a potential squabble with a restaurant on the East Side. Apparently, a place was opening just about the same time as our "Fred's" and had the same name. One day we received a certified letter from a prestigious law firm requesting that we "cease and desist" from using the name "Fred's" for our establishment. The ironic part of this request was the fact that their place was located inside of one of the most pretentious, overpriced retail emporiums in the city, which was located way across town on the East Side. Apparently, the name Fred's was intended to honor the founder of the store. I checked with our lawyers who believed that the request was without merit but cautioned that a battle would be drawn out and expensive. I felt strongly that we should not surrender. I welcomed a well-publicized fight where the highflyers from their lofty perch would descend upon the humble little struggling place on the other side of town. I envisioned tabloid headlines with photos depicting Fred sitting with a hangdog look outside the steps leading down to her little "basement" restaurant versus the goliath retail operation on a fashionable avenue. The photos would be side by side, a picture that money could not buy. The variety of headlines they could place over this scene would be sensational. I'll bet you can think of a few right now. We firmly refused to comply with their lawyer's threat. It seems that these lawyers must have advised their famous clients that it was not a very good idea for them to pick such a sympathetic target. We never heard another word from them.

The second unanticipated development was the fact that we stumbled upon a phrase to go along with a likeness of Fred on our logo and all our printed materials. Of course, when we first opened, there were the usual comments regarding the dog theme and commands such as "come" and "sit" were frequently heard. We decided to formalize the phrase **"Come, Sit, Stay"** as it captured our philosophy. Most restaurants want customers to come, sit down and then leave as soon as possible for the next customer. We wanted to let the public know that we wanted them to hang around and not be rushed... our "gathering place" credo in writing.

"Fred's" opened on a weekday night in late September 1997. We used the time-tested marketing approach. Open the door.

Now, this was crazy ... I started kidding myself that this restaurant business was easy. There I was, a late-blooming novice going into an entirely new business, opening a second place and the customers were streaming in the door. I was astounded. There must have been a whole lot of pent-up demand for the type of places that we had created, because, once again, we were embraced by the neighborhood. Granted, we were small, and it always looked busy, but the sight of a full house with happy customers was as good as it gets. We were far from perfect, kind of like Fred herself, who came up short in her testing as a guide dog. My guess is that people are attracted to enterprises that do not take themselves too seriously but demonstrate all out efforts to please. Soon after opening, we were checked out by the food critic from the NY Times, probably because we were enjoying the initial rush of popularity. His published review was complimentary concerning our cuisine and service. However, he was less enthusiastic about our cramped quarters and the fact that a big gust of wind rushed in every time the front door was opened, which, thankfully, was very often. It was a nice review, but not one that would cause a crush of non-recurring customers. "Fred's" had established a nice beachhead in the neighborhood, and we were anxious to see if we had the staying power to build upon the trust that customers had extended to us.

It turns out that we performed well through the critical first year. This positive experience encouraged us to invest in a minor expansion into an adjoining space. As mentioned earlier, we had lucked out in our relationship with the landlord, and he not only wanted us to have the additional space but agreed to share the expenses involved in the expansion. This development was timely from my standpoint, as another build-out project was of more interest to me than the prospect of being involved in management of the restaurant. Besides, it was day work. It also required having to purchase additional equipment and furnishings, a job I now faced with confidence owing to my experience earned in the rough world of restaurant auctions. As you may have guessed, one of my main objectives was to find another copper-topped bar to be the centerpiece of the expanded space.

By 1998, New York City had perked up from the doldrums that existed in the prior decade. As a result, there were far fewer restaurant closings and auctions. The rare exceptions were places that had just run out of steam after years of operating or where owners were retiring. While looking in the NY Times I happened to see a familiar name that was scheduled for auction. It was the "Pen and Pencil", a well-known saloon that catered to writers, and especially to famous newspaper columnists and celebrities in the news media. It was known as a steak house and gin mill but had actually started in business as a speakeasy during prohibition in the 1920's. Intrigued; I went to the auction. Fortunately, the existing owner, who was a descendant of the family that ran the original speakeasy, was present and he shared some vivid tales of bazaar happenings over a long and colorful lifespan. Apparently, the heydays of the "Pen and Pencil" were the 1940's and the post war era when newspapers were kings and writers, and columnists were the superstars. They all gathered at this little place. As he told his stories, I had visions of these famous members of the fourth estate sitting at the bar engaged in lively, alcohol-fueled discussions about politics and other volatile topics. There were autographed pictures of these celebrities adorning the walls.

Back to the auction ... I had noticed that they had stacked auction items on what appeared to be a bar. When I looked closer, it was indeed a bar, about 14 feet in length. At first glance, the surface of the bar appeared to be copper, but looking closer it was copper pennies, all covered with a high gloss lacquer. Wow! It was not only unique and had an intriguing history, but it was just the right size for our newly expanded space. Again, I lucked out, as there was only one other party bidding owing to the bar's small size. There was no way I was going to lose this war. We paid a very fair price and ended up with a prize. To this day, the bar is proudly featured in "Fred's", and more penny-adorned sections have been added. I had always believed that it was important to house our place in an older building to capture some of the history and tradition that made this such a great city. Having a piece of one of the city's most notorious saloons comfortably sitting in our little place meant that we were being faithful to our mission.

Things were going almost too smoothly. It all related to the outcome of my idealistic game plan which called for entrusting stewardship of a new place to young professionals. My instincts and prior experience told me that the plan was sound, but the actual results were a big gamble. The young partner I had selected turned out to be perfect for the job. I saw his solid work ethic in action during the build-out as we labored with tough challenges. Once we opened, his personality was a good match for the task of greeting customers and setting a casual, comfortable atmosphere. He also actually listened to this old guy when I suggested that he should surround himself with strong people. He hired a manager who was not only talented but also totally embraced our concept and philosophy. By adding this strong individual, my partner was able to enjoy the luxury of delegation, an absolute necessity in the pressure of running a business that grinds up owners and never stops for breath 364 days a year. Our partnership was solid to the degree that enabled us to expand "Fred's" on two occasions, once for the addition that housed the little copper penny bar and then another modest expansion of the barroom. These expenditures would never have gone forward without a comfort level that we would be around for years. However, smooth sailing sometimes can breed complacency and its cousin, boredom, may join the party. These two unlikely companions did creep into lives and should have been treated as good things brought about by hard work. However, we learned that, in the hands of very active people, they can be very bad traits that can lead to all kinds of trouble. For instance, thinking about opening a branch of "Fred's". By our third year, we had settled into a rhythm that was nice, but not challenging. We started talking with our chef about the possibility of opening another "Fred's" on the East Side. Like the cockeyed optimists that we were, it was deemed a no brainer. This statement leads me to a detour to tell you about restaurant Number 3. As promised, we will return to talk more about the original "Fred's" because it rightfully is the star in this story.

The timing was 2000, my 64th year. I thought that I had enough pizzazz left for this project. I was wrong. I should have known by this age that, to be energized, you must totally believe in the undertaking. Not that I didn't believe in the concept of "Fred's". Quite the opposite. We had proof that it works. However, I was never comfortable with the East Side as a home for our type of place nor would it be easy to find space that would meet our criteria for comfort and cost. These concerns added up to less than 100% enthusiasm and energy. Not a great beginning. We looked at many potential sites, with no luck. We finally found a spot on Third Avenue (at 92nd Street) that was an existing Irish bar that was in the process of transforming itself into a sports bar. Obviously, there was some dissent among their partners about the wisdom of this decision, so they were entertaining the option of selling their lease and contents. Now, you may have heard of the expression "turnkey" when sellers describe their sterling asset. It is designed to lure the uninitiated into thinking that the new owner just walks in, puts his people in place, and starts up business the next day. The owners of this establishment made such a representation. I am here to swear that no such condition exists and certainly not in their place. However, they did have a very good lease, and this was the major factor in our decision to make a deal. After going through the ordeal of receiving the landlord's agreement to accept us as tenants and then fighting through NYC's red tape, the renovation and redesign became my responsibility.

This was a tough assignment. Aside from an old-world mahogany bar, the place was too large and lacking any character whatsoever. I spent long days trying to put lipstick on this hog. The neighborhood was sterile, comprised of surrounding high-rise buildings with very little pedestrian traffic and few shoppers. A number of passerby's would stick their head in the door to see what was going on and quite a few of them offered comforting statements like ... "good luck, this spot is a big problem ...it changes hands every few years". Nice. These wonderful people had a big impact on my attitude. Rather than struggling with a project that I had reservations about, it became a mission to convert these negative neighbors into believers. We all worked hard to make the place as comfortable as its cross-town namesake.

The first year of "Fred's" operations on the East Side can best be described as mixed. Volume was moderate, but the stretching of resources between two restaurants proved to be a problem. It was a concern that we had discussed and anticipated, but the reality of everyday pressures on both places placed a damper on our normal upbeat approach. Our chef had been the key instigator in going forward with the project and he indicated that he would be willing to take over the East Side operation. This was fine, except he did not have the resources for such a commitment. This meant that he had to seek other partners and backers. Again, this was OK, but because these parties would be unknown to my partner and myself, we decided that it would not be prudent to let them use our well-established name for the restaurant. The chef decided to operate under another name. In keeping with restaurant traditions in the city, this facility only lasted several years.

Meanwhile "Fred's" kept chugging along over there on the other side of town. In her early, or shakeout, years there were really no dramatic episodes or crisis situations other than the normal abnormal things that go on in our business. Oddly, we did have an unusual number of celebrities as customers. This may have been attributed, once again, to our laid-back atmosphere and the fact that we were a safe harbor from pestering fans. They also may have been dog lovers and there were some pictures of their very own dogs up on our walls. I do remember a special occasion when my wife, June, and I were enjoying a night out, including dinner at "Fred's". When we entered, we were astounded to see that the place was stark empty. Not a soul, except our staff. After awhile, one foursome did enter and make their way into the dining room. They had their choice of tables. A movie company had been filming in the neighborhood, and I happened to recognize Nora Ephron, who was the author and director of the film *"You've Got Mail."* We had a nice conversation and she wondered about the absence of our usual phalanx of customers. So did we. Apparently, the last episode of the Jerry Seinfeld Show was going on the air that night. It created a phenomenon similar to a blackout. No one left their apartments. We did have one customer at the bar who entered just in time to view the episode on our barroom TV. It was Tom Hanks, who was co-staring in Nora's movie. We learned the next day that virtually every restaurant in the city was empty all because of what turned out to be a dreadful Seinfeld episode, providing a poor ending to an otherwise great series.

Then came September 11, 2001.

I don't know if I'm up to the task of describing the depth of the impact that this day had on our lives. Our personal experience was marginal compared to the thousands of tragedies and heartaches sustained by victims and their families. If you happened to watch any of the documentaries or ceremonies marking every anniversary of 9/11, you surely must have felt the incredible degree of sorrow and loss that haunts all the survivors to this day. I am going to tell you our story, if only to relate how fragile and resilient we all are and how the slim margin of fate was in control that awful day. June worked as a lawyer for New York City. Her office was less than two blocks from the World Trade Center. As part of a physical therapy routine for an injured shoulder, on her way to work several days a week she went to swim in a pool at a health club located at the Downtown Marriott Hotel. This club was located on the 22nd floor of the Marriott, a building that was sandwiched between the twin towers. She normally arrived at the club around 8 a.m. and then walked through the World Trade Center to her office by 9 a.m.

On that Tuesday she had finished her swim and was waiting for the elevator in the lobby on the 22nd floor around 15 minutes before 9 a.m. Suddenly, all the picture windows in the lobby imploded, sending glass everywhere. This was followed by a loud crash as a large piece of concrete came down through the ceiling not more than five feet from where June was standing. It was from the impact of the first plane. No one knew what was happening, but it was so bizarre that the first thought was to avoid getting on the elevator. June, along with just about everyone on the 22nd floor, headed for the stairway and began to rush down the stairs to somehow get to ground level. She arrived at the first floor and ran out onto the street. Again, no one knew what had caused the explosion, and officials were speculating that a plane had hit the North Tower in error. It was then that June saw the second plane circling over the harbor. It came right over her, flying low and fast before it hit the second tower, smashing into the building with huge flames and black smoke immediately engulfing the area. All of the people who had gotten to street level then began to run south, toward Battery Park, located at the tip of Manhattan. None of the cell phones were working, but June managed to find a small shoe repair store and the kind people there let her use their phone. She got through to me and tried to describe her situation. The only thing she knew by then, because of the 2nd plane, was the fact that this had to have been the work of terrorists. She was totally broken up about the loss of innocent lives and used language to describe their heinous act in terms that I had never heard from her lips. She still had no idea of the unimaginable extent of the damage and even suggested that she could circle around and somehow get to her office. I used much stronger language to tell her to get out of the entire area and work her way east and north. She agreed. That was our only communication for the next few hours.

My experience at home was vastly different, but I'm sure was typical of hundreds of thousands of human beings whose loved ones were in harm's way and were watching hell erupt on their televisions. I knew exactly where June would have been in that timeframe, somewhere between the health club and her office, maybe even at work slightly early. I called her office only to learn that she had not arrived. Panic and total helplessness set in. I called the kids, telling them that Mom may be in the middle of this nightmare. This horrible stretch of time, which seemed like an eternity, ended with June's call from the shoe repair shop. The only remaining uncertainty was whether or not June would honor my very strong advice to leave the area. It took about an hour for the towers to start falling, so there was a second period of helplessness, not knowing her whereabouts. We finally made contact several hours later and called our kids to talk and cry. Fate played its cruel hand that day for 2,796 souls and their families and friends. Our family was lucky. Were it not for a few seconds in timing either way or if June had decided to take an elevator that would have surely been disabled and destroyed, the outcome would have been unthinkable. It was unvarnished hell for everyone.

The ripple effect of 9/11 was unprecedented. No one knew how to respond or behave. Obviously, after the initial shock and disbelief, one of the first gut reactions is to want to help. But how? There were no outlets for these emotions. "Fred's" manager called me soon after learning the news, seeking advice. Should we open or remain closed out of respect? My immediate response was that we definitely should open, but it would be completely inappropriate to operate as a business. We should offer free coffee and comfort. I believed that most people were feeling lost and confused. What was paramount was a need to somehow get in touch with loved ones and friends. New York City, despite its size and reputation, has neighborhoods and networks that act almost like small towns. "Fred's" turned out to be a place for people to gather, exchange information and to hug and cry. Our decision to remain open as a gathering place was entirely in keeping with the role that we had always espoused ... being a safe harbor. Throughout the city, the days that followed were filled with efforts to somehow help the work being done at the site. We organized customers to help prepare food to send down to workers. Our role during this time was miniscule in relation to all the efforts that were being exerted. If we provided even one ounce of comfort, we did the right thing.

I must apologize for the poor chronology in this story. This flaw is mostly because the story is based entirely on recollection, an asset that has sustained some serious wear and tear. Opening all these restaurants hasn't helped. After looking back at what has been written so far, there are concerns that I may have lost you with all the jumping around. I will now go forward to the very last restaurant, with a promise to go back to my final thoughts on "Fred's". I will also try to explain why I began to write this story in the first place.

Forward to age 70. I finally got around to opening a restaurant that honored one of the industry's finest traditions ... it failed. Restaurant No.4 was probably doomed from the start. However, those kinds of negative thoughts never entered my mind once I started on a project. The location was wrong, the economy was wrong, and the demographics, whatever they are, were very wrong. Also, there weren't any solid candidates to run the place and then take ownership. A basic building block of my plan was missing. Given all these negatives, why would any sane person go forward? Here, the motivation was unusual. My normal drive has been to create a gathering place for the benefit of customers, with a secondary consideration of housing the place in an older building to capture the atmosphere. In this instance, the primary inspiration was a sad, sad abandoned building. It sat on the main street of the village that we called home in a beautiful section of the Western Catskill Mountains. (Note: Remember, way back, I mentioned that we might move to this town. Well, we did.) This building was an eyesore of unrivaled magnitude. When you drove into the village, it dominated your vision and almost made you turn around and leave, thinking that bad things must be afoot. It was an embarrassment to the community.

June then purchased a solo practice law firm in the village and was exerting the long hours that good lawyers tend to do. I was left to my own devices, a bad place. I had always daydreamed about doing something for the community because it had fallen so far from its lofty perch and was not handling the demotion well. I started looking around for a project. A young builder from downstate had just purchased the downtrodden, sad building on Main Street. I met with him. Dumb meets Dumber. His idealism and enthusiasm were impressive. He was going to take the biggest sow within 100 miles and turn it into a silk purse. To make this viable, he needed a gullible tenant, someone who would march with him into this battle against blight. That's me. This turned out to be my first bad decision. The builder was in over his head, had an inexperienced crew and the building itself held many secret flaws that came to light each day. The result of all this chaos was inevitable cost overruns which triggered fights with his partners who were still located downstate and had no idea of the magnitude of the problems. Like a jerk, I stuck with the program and somehow managed to build a restaurant on the first floor of the building, including the installation of a brand-new kitchen, refrigeration, and ventilation system. This was a very expensive investment with absolutely no chance of even breaking even.

If the torture of living through a chaotic restoration project wasn't enough, the actual opening and running of the restaurant was even worse. Sure, people did pour into the place, prompted by curiosity, good food and a nice barroom with a penny-topped bar. The honeymoon lasted less than a year. As feared, the big problem was the absence of talented managerial staff and a slim field of experienced wait staff. I had hired a young man as manager, and while he had the right resume there was always a concern about his maturity and stability. Well, after about three months he managed to show why my concerns were justified. He liked to extend the hours of operation so he could enjoy all the stuff that went on during normal hours. This was not going to work out. My reliance on strong professional management in all my prior restaurants gave me comfort and confidence. Here, the absence of these assets made each day a struggle. I finally realized that the only option was to find some outside parties to buy the business. These efforts were not successful. I handed over the keys to the landlord and wished him good luck. I understand that a restaurant has recently been opened and the building is being kept in good condition. While the decision to open a place was irrational for a number of reasons, I did appreciate the first year when customers were plentiful and appreciated the effort that went into opening a decent restaurant. But, by far, the most gratifying outcome was the fact that the restoration of that old, sad building turned out to provide an incentive for other people to make investments towards restoring the village to its former glory. As you know, I love to start things rolling, and what would normally be considered a misadventure was, in fact, a good thing for a community that needed to believe in itself once again.

Back to "Fred's" in the Big Apple. It's good to return to this little island of comfort on Amsterdam Avenue. I recently learned that my original partner believed it was time to pass ownership on to new proprietors. These owners apparently are keeping the name "Fred's" along with the theme and spirit as established. The year 2023 marks 27 years of operation. Their decision to continue with the founding mission is great news!

Once I decided to write, why did I elect to write about my unconventional activities after age 55? Well, there were two important reasons. One was to honor the memory of Fred, as she inspired the creation of "Fred's". The other purpose was to talk about Guiding Eyes for the Blind and the outstanding work that they do every day. They deserve our ongoing support.

The restaurant business proved to be mysterious like the phony Wizard of Oz, misunderstood like most politicians and mismanaged almost all the time, like my last endeavor. Despite these traits, my experiences were funny, challenging, exhausting and, surprisingly, very gratifying.

Where else can you have such a ride? It was good to have you along.

Graffiti on Columbus Avenue – The norm in 1990.

A building is reborn (sorry, pink umbrella was free).

Phoebe .... inspiration during construction.

The Crazy House-in-a-Resturant, certainly unmatched in NYC.

Love at first sight …. an ugly bamboo hut. A perfect home for Fred's.

The new entrance featuring a welcoming Fred.

The ugly interior corner, with a dark painting of Singapore Sally on the wall.

Discovery of beautiful brickwork and fireplace under sheetrock.

The same corner in next phase, before all the customers' dog pictures.

Bar with copper pennies, including partial dog pictures.

The sad building on Main Street, spoiling an historic mountain village.

Fred's gift.

One More Thought...

I've been trying to understand why it became so important to start writing at such a late stage in life. The only thought that kept emerging was a desire to express gratitude. To be thankful for everything from family to fulfillment. Why was I so grateful? The answer surfaced... because I have been experiencing love. This magical gift arrived when I first met June over 63 years ago. Then came more love with Mark and Marly and five grandchildren. Does it get any better? It doesn't seem possible, but these treasures also came with an unsuspected dividend. You gain a sense of security. Once grounded, you have the degree of confidence to open your inner thoughts.

So now I know the answer ... It was love that made me write.

· notes ·

· notes ·

· notes ·

· notes ·